The Bible, the Church and Homosexuality

The Bible, the Church and Homosexuality

Edited by
NICHOLAS COULTON
Foreword by
THE RIGHT REVEREND RICHARD HARRIES,
BISHOP OF OXFORD

DARTON·LONGMAN + TODD

First published in 2005 by
Darton, Longman and Todd Ltd
1 Spencer Court
140–142 Wandsworth High Street
London
SW18 4JJ

ISBN 0 232 52606 0

A catalogue record for this book is available from the British
Library.

Phototypeset by IntypeLibra Ltd, London
Printed and bound in Great Britain by
CPI Bath

Contents

Notes on Contributors

MARILYN MCCORD ADAMS is Regius Professor of Divinity and a Canon of Christ Church, Oxford. She specialises in medieval and philosophical theology, has published a book on William Ockham, and *Horrendous Evils and the Goodness of God*, is working on a systematic Christology, and has published numerous articles in these fields. She is ordained in the Episcopal Church USA and served parishes in Los Angeles during the AIDS epidemic in the 1980s, where she became involved in issues of human sexuality and the Church.

ROBERT MERRIHEW ADAMS is a Senior Research Fellow of Mansfield College, Oxford, and Visiting Professor of Philosophy in the University of Oxford. He taught philosophy of religion, moral philosophy, contemporary metaphysics, and the history of modern philosophy for thirty-five years at the University of Michigan, UCLA and Yale University. His most recent book is *Finite and Infinite Goods: A framework for ethics*. He is a minister of the Presbyterian Church USA.

MARGARET BEDGGOOD is Professor of Law at the University of Waikato, New Zealand, a member of the International Executive Committee of Amnesty International, and an Anglican Third-Order Franciscan. She was formerly the Chief Commissioner of the New Zealand Human Rights Commission and a member of the (NZ) Anglican Pakeha Commission on Sexuality. She teaches on the Oxford Human Rights Summer School every year, and on the Oxford Theology summer school periodically.

NICHOLAS COULTON is Sub-Dean of Christ Church, Oxford and formerly Dean of Newcastle. He is on the Executive of the Association of English Cathedrals, a Governor of Ripon College Cuddesdon, a member of the Legal Advisory Commission of the Church of England, and was until this year a Director of the Ecclesiastical Insurance Group. He is a qualified solicitor. He was a member of the General Synod between 1985 and 1990 (at the time of the Higton debate) and more recently, representing the Northern Deans, between 1998 and 2002.

JOHN DRURY is Fellow and Chaplain of All Souls, Oxford and from 1991 to 2003 was Dean of Christ Church. He has written about St Luke's gospel and the parables in the gospels. His most recent book is *Painting the Word: Christian pictures and their meanings* (Yale). He is at present working on the poetry of George Herbert.

CHRISTOPHER ROWLAND has been Dean Ireland Professor of the Exegesis of Holy Scripture in Oxford University and a Fellow of The Queen's College, Oxford, since 1991. He has written widely on the Book of Revelation and the centrality of apocalypticism in the study of the New Testament. He is at present working on a book on William Blake and the Bible.

JANE SHAW is Dean of Divinity, Chaplain and Fellow of New College, Oxford, and teaches theology and history in the University. She was the Theological Consultant to the House of Bishops' working party on Human Sexuality, which produced the recent report *Some Issues in Human Sexuality: A guide to the debate.* She is co-editor (with Harriet Harris) of *The Call for Women Bishops* (SPCK). She is at present writing the history of a modern British millenarian community.

Foreword

When we are being unreflective, it is easy to assume that Christian beliefs and attitudes have remained much the same down the ages. As soon as we look at the evidence, however, we are aware of sharp, sometimes startling, differences of understanding between one age and the next. The Medieval Church, for example, was dominated by the fear of hell, as we see in the great 'dooms' depicted in our churches. The preoccupations of the Church today are very different. This specially commissioned collection of essays brings out well how our understanding of gender and sexuality has differed from age to age. If we are to avoid being at the mercy of attitudes in our own time, whether conservative or progressive, some awareness of the historical dimension is vital.

In all this flux, where do we find the fundamentals? Can we find them at all, or do they slip through our fingers as we strip away each reinterpretation to discover another skin of reinterpretation below that? The authors, deeply committed to discovering the truth of Christ for our own times, believe that we can, humbly, reach after that truth. Scholars, all with Oxford connections, they seek to take us beyond the clichés and stereotyped positions. Faithful to the Bible, they want us to see that the Bible has to be reinterpreted afresh in every age and that there are issues now that the Church cannot avoid. T. S. Eliot believed that any poet who was going to continue writing after the age of thirty needed to do so with the whole history of European literature in his bones. As such, he was the most traditional of all modern poets. Yet, he, more than anyone, is a modern poet par excellence, with an acute awareness of the times in which he wrote. It was his profound sense of tradition that enabled him to be so sensitive and truthful in responding to his own time. This is of course very different from traditionalism, which is simply repeating the truths which came out of very different circumstances in the past. So it is that the authors of this book are equally concerned to be faithful to Christians of previous generations and true to our own times. They combine a deep understanding of the past with a passion to communicate the message of Christ faithfully today.

Richard Oxon
January 2005

Introduction

Far more people today than forty years ago are aware of the existence of homosexuals, if not within their own families, at least within close acquaintanceship circles. Furthermore, there are others who find themselves more able to be aware of their same-sex desires in a way that was impossible in earlier decades.

There is also a growing conviction among those who know themselves to be fundamentally homosexual that their nature, with its same-sex desires, is how they are made in the image of God; and further, that when their desires find fulfilment in faithful loving relationships, they are as much within the purposes of God as are faithful committed heterosexuals making love.

For many loyal Christians this presents a confusing and sometimes painful dilemma. Their hearts and friendships may lead them to want to give support and affirmation, and indeed to celebrate when the person they know has found love in a long-term partnership – or, if they fall in love with a person of the same sex, to commit to that relationship wholeheartedly. On the other hand, if they are told that the Scriptures are unequivocal in condemning any physical expression of homosexual love, or even the orientation itself, or when they see official Church policies drawing lines as if this were the case, then they feel that they have no choice. The Scriptures must be the final arbiter. But is that really the message of Scripture?

These essays are written for those who find themselves in that dilemma. The essayists write in the conviction that there are other ways for Christians properly to engage with

1

the Scriptures, and that there are several other important considerations, under God, as we approach this subject.

The issues

What then are the issues for the Church, and how do the essays in this book relate to them?

One issue is the authority of Scripture and how Christians today are to weigh it alongside what they believe they see of the Spirit working, both in the Church and in the world. Christopher Rowland's essay looks at this in depth.

Second, there is the way in which human societies across the world have invented differing institutions to channel or control sexual expression. Marilyn McCord Adams' essay explores how institutions respond when taboos start to change.

Third, Jane Shaw describes how the Church's attitudes to sexuality, marriage, celibacy and related questions have shifted dramatically over the course of 2000 years, and therefore asks how we locate our current debate about sexuality within the history of those attitudes.

Margaret Bedggood brings a Human Rights perspective, not as a discipline which is in some way secular and separate or even opposed to Christian teaching on daily responsibility, but as an approach which has partly at least grown out of Christian doctrine on what it is to be human.

Ideas of what is natural or unnatural are often invoked in discussion of ethical issues about sexuality. Raising the question whether anything that appears in nature can really be unnatural, Robert Merrihew Adams explores the relevance of theological ideas of creation and fall, and the first two chapters of Genesis. He suggests that a Christian concept of vocation may provide a more comprehensively adequate framework for thinking about the ethical issues.

John Drury distinguishes between claims to be converted to Christianity and really being so, between being human and being humane. He considers the temptation for religious groups, newly converted or with a strong sense of being 'within the covenant', to see their views as central to reality with room for no other.

2

The first essay, by Nicholas Coulton, describes the way in which the ground of debate, particularly within the Church of England, has been shifting in recent years. He introduces the many-faceted subject in general, starting with a word about the Bible, which Christopher Rowland will later consider in greater detail.

© 2005 Nicholas Coulton

1 Does it matter enough, and to whom?

Nicholas Coulton

Taking the Bible whole

What are Christians to make of the Scriptures? Is it that the Bible should be read by Christians as if the whole ground plan of lifelong heterosexual monogamy can be discovered from the three opening chapters of the Old Testament book of Genesis, with their accounts of creation and the fall of Adam? That is the starting-point for *Some Issues in Human Sexuality*, the guide to the debate published by the House of Bishops in 2003.[1] Their conclusions follow along that pre-set line. But does not the new revelation in Jesus Christ give a starting-point which is dramatically different, so that the Old Testament falls into a different perspective?

Not only do Genesis 1 and 2 present different accounts of creation (drawing on different Near Eastern materials, and at different stages in Israelite history), they are now read by some Christians and Jews as advocating a social equality between men and women which would not have been recognised in most of the intervening patriarchal centuries. What relationship between men and women is to be understood by Eve's being created from Adam's rib? Is it a relationship of female inferiority and dependence upon man, or is it one of identity and unity marking out human companionship distinct from other animals? And does the long history of Jewish interpretation of their Scriptures (*midrash*) offer any help to Christians wrestling with the literal meaning of individual texts? It is sometimes claimed that Jews (and indeed Moslems) have a straightforward literalist view of scriptural texts and are affronted by Christian attempts to reinterpret them. However, within Orthodox

4

Judaism there is a debate whether Leviticus 18:22 (the principal text quoted on homosexuality) is not more to do with sexual domination than with homosexuality as such.

In several areas of life most people have long ago accepted principles contrary to what can be read out of Scripture. Deeper questions arising from this are often sidestepped. How are Christians to treat a Bible which applauds Israelite genocide of neighbouring Canaanites or, in its psalms, the beating out of the brains of Babylonian babies? How shall they regard a Bible which condemns the usury on which the western world's wealth creation is built? How shall they interpret a New Testament which insists that women in church shall be veiled and silent, or which endorses slavery as an unchallenged fact of life? How are issues of a 'Just War' or of God's promise of the land to Israel to be understood in a very changed international context?

A responsible attitude to the Bible does not ignore some parts and highlight others. The Bible, and for Christians the Christ of the Bible, must be taken more seriously than that – which is very different from saying that each verse in isolation, or those which suit our personal agenda, must be given the status of divine command. And, in the context of taking the Bible whole, there are some parts – the genocide instructions, for instance – which Christian conscience would say no longer have any moral force, if they ever had. They are now seen as intolerable, and contrary to the purposes of God as understood through Jesus Christ.

The seriousness which is needed, not least since 11 September 2001, is one which lets modern science, history and psychology influence our beliefs as much as our tradition of rituals, symbols and stories, so that we can converse with those in Islam and in other faiths who are helping their religions to make a similar journey. There are those in Islam and in Orthodox Judaism who are working in that way, so it will not do simply to claim that a modern or 'enlightened' attitude to sexuality puts the Church at the mercy of other religions. The essays in this book offer a basis on which such discussions with other faiths could take place.

5

Why all the fuss?

Some suggest that homosexuality is too small a matter for the Church to concern itself with, compared (say) with the huge scale of world poverty. Is it sufficiently important to justify its being the cause of schism in the Church?

Awareness of homosexuals in our own close circles is only a partial indication of the degree of incidence. Calculations normally suggest that between 5 per cent and 10 per cent, even 15 per cent, of the male population either is homosexual or has had homosexual experiences. The percentage for female homosexuals is similarly imprecise. Government policy-makers in Britain take 6 per cent as their estimate of gay population in calculating, for instance, the likely cost of civil registration of gay partnerships. That would suggest nearly 1 million men and 1 million women. The fact that in the 2001 census for England and Wales only 78,522 were willing to declare themselves as living in a gay or lesbian relationship raises important questions. Those in a relationship will be substantially fewer than those who know themselves to be gay. But many who are gay will have been afraid to declare themselves so.

The biggest-ever Gay Pride march in London, in 1993, was attended by 300,000 people. Again that will have included only a small percentage of those in the United Kingdom who know they are gay.

It is noteworthy that nearly all the 78,522 declaring in the census that they are couples come from southern England together with Blackpool and Manchester. Other than that, north of a line from Bristol to London, few were willing to declare themselves in partnership. The numbers of those not in a stable relationship will be much greater.

Not all, whether male or female, have found it possible to be 'out' in their home communities. Large numbers have found refuge in the anonymity of cities, but the predominant southern bias of the census return (of couples only) suggests that across the northern part of England there are many who are either not coupled or, even if coupled, still not declared.

An increasing number these days find themselves able to demonstrate their existence in the public arena through the various Pride marches, and on an everyday level, for example visibility in the workplace, but there remain many for whom public demonstrations are either more than they dare risk or quite at odds with their instinctive modesty and style of behaviour. The suicide statistics quoted later in this essay indicate the levels of pressure, and indeed cruelty, encountered or feared. Physical attacks on homosexuals occur frequently and are not always reported. What is perceived to be the Church's official disapproval of homosexuality lends encouragement and sanction to such attacks.

Where tolerance, fairness and incidences of cruelty are concerned, does it matter whether the true number of homosexuals in England and Wales is 100,000 or 300,000 or 3 million?

What is said here about England and Wales applies also in other countries. Nor is homosexuality, as is sometimes suggested, merely a western phenomenon. Same-sex desires have been acknowledged in all periods of history and in cultures across the globe.

God's work

A sexuality which has to hide itself is demeaning and destructive of the person. Acceptance, by oneself and by others, is needed for integration, wholeness and fulfilment in human relationships. A minority, not deviant but different, will only find fulfilment with people of the same gender. Concealment is alien to Christian understanding of the God who rejoices in those made in God's likeness. It is like Adam in the Garden of Eden, in shame hiding his nakedness. God's work in creation is to make and keep us human, that is, to help us become persons in relationship with others, able to love and to give ourselves in love. Included in that humanity is our being sexual persons in love. One understanding of that creation story is that, cast out of the Garden, Adam was no longer programmed to obey God but, with free will, had to work out who he was and what adult relationship entailed.

The emphasis is on **giving**: not everyone will find one other to whom they can completely give themselves; there

7

are, as there have always been, those who find their fulfilment in giving themselves only through generosity of relationship and service to a diversity of people rather than through a deeply personal relationship with one, and in finding the One in the many. The form of service may be professional or voluntary or in a thorough-going orientation of life; their giving may never have sexual (or genital) expression, but achieves a completeness not the less.

The question remains whether, when there is sexual expression, it is only those who are able to give themselves lovingly to those of different gender who are able to become that complete human whom God intends. In an article as long ago as 1979[2] Rowan Williams (now Archbishop) helpfully identified the sexual relation as one in which **power** is given up; while power is given up in many relationships, in the sexual relation our bodies with their distinctive separateness are both surrendered and accepted, and with acceptance comes affirmation. Our bodies are so powerfully a sign of our independent being, of our boundaries, that to be accepted and valued as other is powerful affirmation. To commit that surrender into fidelity transforms a solitary act into a relationship within which grace, forgiveness and acceptance have the opportunity to work. Fidelity, faithfulness, is an aspect of the grace of acceptance, a response to gift received. That surrender and acceptance are intrinsic to our creation as sexual beings.

Harry Williams in *Soundings*, a book of essays by Cambridge theologians in 1962,[3] used the illustration of the Greek film *Never on Sunday* in which a prostitute in the Piraeus gives herself to a young sailor who is afraid, nervous and on edge, not because he thinks he is embarking on something wicked, but because he distrusts his capacity for physical union. The prostitute gives him confidence and self-respect and he goes away a deeper fuller person than he came in. Harry Williams saw the prostitute as doing an act of charity, proclaiming the glory of God, equipping the man as he was not before. Rowan Williams in his article seventeen years later does not seem to deny that, but raises the concept of faithfulness as a more extended context within which grace may work. He raises the poignant question how within 'the complex and often tortured world of sexual relationships today, people are to learn about sex-as-grace when, for no fault of theirs, the institutional shape of faithful mutuality is not available for them' and he adds in parenthesis 'and this does not only apply to homosexuals'. It is not exactly that there is a standard which they cannot 'satisfy'; there is a certain embodiment which is socially denied them.

Changing attitudes to the physical

Recent years have seen much change in public attitudes to touch and intimacy. A culture of anxiety about male homosexuality meant, and for some still means, that many predominantly heterosexual men have not let themselves love those of their own sex as fully as they might, and so a great many boys and men grew up starved of a range of affections which might help them respond in a more demonstrative way to either sex.

Changes in liturgy and manners have enabled many in the churches to experience much greater closeness, particularly but not only in the sharing of the Peace. The parallel liturgies of football and other sports have made a ritual of physical intimacy with patterns of celebration unthinkable some sixty years ago – though earlier eras again were in some circumstances less restrained or anxious about physical contact.

The price of liberation

Alongside changes in social attitude have gone changes in the law. By the Sexual Offences Act of 1967, in England and Wales homosexual behaviour between consenting adults in private became no longer a criminal offence. That step had taken Parliament ten years since the Wolfenden Committee's recommendations of 1957.

For many homosexual people the change in English law, coinciding with change in other countries, came as liberation. They could come out of the closet, openly acknowledge partnerships and practice, and feel new confidence in being who they believed themselves to be.

9

For many, particularly in big cities, changing public attitudes have brought acceptance and a naturalness of life. For many others, attitudes have been slow to change: local hostility may even have deepened, violent attacks have been a frequent threat, and the close family unit has been retained only at the price of secrecy and fear. Paradoxically those unable to share their secret with parents, siblings, spouses or children, have felt greater isolation in these decades of official liberation, and the number who have felt driven in the end to suicide remains tragically high.

Several studies across the world in the last twenty years (USA, Canada, Belgium, New Zealand, Australia) indicate that young male homosexuals are several times more at risk of self-harm or suicide than young male heterosexuals. Some studies suggest that 78 per cent of first attempts at suicide occur between the ages of twelve and sixteen. It appears that homosexually oriented males may well account for more than half of the male youth deaths resulting from suicide. In some studies the percentages are actually underestimated, because the proportion of homosexuals in the population has been overestimated.

If figures of this kind are correct, what are the implications for a culture in which many young people find it so difficult to tell others that they think they may be gay, and in which popular prejudices against homosexuality are reinforced by messages coming out from Christian Churches?

Ambivalent media attitudes have played a part in this with, as it were, one law for those in certain walks of life, another for those seen as vulnerable to public exposure.

Film stars have to some extent felt free to 'come out' – though the HIV/AIDS explosion in the 1980s for a time pushed this process into reverse. British television companies by contrast have been more cautious about owning the homosexuality of some of their public figures. Documentary dramas, soap operas and films have tentatively introduced issues of homosexuality. Sit-coms with gay characters have won large ratings on the screens. However, alongside that, as a recent documentary demonstrated, TV authorities have consistently suppressed any acknowledgement of homosexuality in, for instance, comedians and game-show hosts, for fear that it might rebound with unpopularity and falling ratings. Their homosexuality has been a guilty secret, well known within the media circle but hidden from the public arena.

Changes in the law have not ended mockery, vindictiveness and prejudice at work. Alongside the growth in tolerance has gone a growth in hostility, with outbreaks from time to time of 'queer bashing'. The changes in law and in culture produced in the Church of England debates a Puritan backlash, which has made single clergy more conspicuous and more vulnerable, whether homosexual or not.

A vital call

Amidst all this the Church of England and other Churches have been struggling to find a way. A succession of reports and debates has pointed in one direction or another. The published material has reached considerable proportions. A brief review of this shifting debate is set out in the Appendix. The task now is to get its findings into parts of the Church which have not so far shared in the debates for which the Church has called. Issues of sexuality reach right across the Church. They touch many families, individuals and friendships within the mainstream Church, on its fringes and amongst those who have felt obliged to distance themselves from the institutional Church.

Here are issues of mission and ministry, of pastoral care and of doctrine, which must not simply be left to decisions of Church synods and hierarchies. It is Christians in their secular lives as well as in their churches who, by words and actions and by what they leave undone, are seen to express the mind of the Church, even the mind of Christ.

It is vitally important that as many Christians as possible engage in the debate. They are needed both to take part in the continuing engagement with Scripture and doctrine and to hear prayerfully and respectfully the voices of those who have been reticent about speaking aloud what they have believed to be their experience of God's love and of the pain which has come to them along with it.

11

It is for this wider sharing of the issues that the present book is written.

A deeper music

Too readily does the debate polarise into those who hold fast to what they believe is the (only) message of the Scriptures and those who are categorised as 'liberals', following an agenda which might in turn be categorised as 'keeping up with the world'. In truth, the so-called 'liberals' include many who believe that the Scriptures provide other major narratives which have as much right to be taken seriously as those which are dominated by the Genesis accounts of creation and fall, and also liberals who believe that taking what is known of Jesus as the starting-point offers a radically different way of understanding God and God's will for humankind.

Far from simply dancing to the world's tune, authentic liberalism (with liberal Catholicism and liberal evangelism) listens both to the centuries' ebb and flow of the Church's tradition and to what it detects of the Spirit working in today's world beyond the Church's boundaries, and tries to discern beneath both the deeper music and calling of God's voice.[4]

This is not to say that Jesus sits light to law: he does not, and his words at the beginning of the Sermon on the Mount make clear how seriously he takes it but, as Professor Keith Ward demonstrates in *God: A guide for the perplexed*,[5] the Acts of the Apostles (particularly chapters 10 and 15) shows the Early Church discovering with some difficulty where the deep and inward keeping of ancient law departs from its rigid application. When Jesus endorsed the Old Testament he did so not as a revelation complete in itself but, as Archbishop Michael Ramsey taught, 'as a first volume in relation to which he was himself the second volume'.[6]

There are also those categorised as 'liberals', who believe that the Holy Spirit working in and through the world may be God's way of bringing the Church to find a deeper truth in what it has taken in a literalist sense. Professor Ward in the same book[7] comments that,

It would be a great mistake to think that Jews, even the most Orthodox, take the commandments literally. The rules are more like a set of precedents which rabbis can adapt to changing circumstances, declare obsolete, or re-interpret – but never ignore . . . Ironically, although some Christians accuse Jews of being 'legalistic', it is often the Christians who are more legalistic about the written texts than Jewish rabbis, who see the statutes and ordinances as bases for rigorous discussion, frequent disagreement and ever-expanding debate about what God requires.

The few scriptural texts which are taken to refer to homosexuality may seem at first sight to be clear and categorical, yet all of them have been questioned by recent Jewish and Christian scholarship. Read within their own contexts and circumstances, if anything about them is clear it is that they do not refer to a faithful sexual union between those of the same gender: that kind of loving relationship between people who would never find their wholeness and completion in heterosexual marriage is not a circumstance that the biblical writers could have contemplated within the thought-forms of their day. Again, later essays in this book pursue these questions of the handling of Scripture.

How the world changes

Leaving aside those few scriptural texts, there is a bigger debate altogether. To understand the Bible as fundamentally the rule-book of fixed and unchanging law is a very different approach from seeing it as the fallible record of where previous generations reached in understanding the nature of their relationship with God.

In the history of science at fairly frequent intervals one way of understanding has had to be abandoned and replaced by another. This is called a paradigm shift. A critical understanding of the writing of the Bible requires us also to be honest in facing changes of emphasis not only in morality, but in a wide range of approaches to be found in different cultures and the shifting arrangements and understanding about gender-role. Until very recently, as witnessed for example in the emergence of women as business partners in secular working life, the model under-standing of what partnership meant were same-sex alliances. In these could ideally be found qualities of benevolence, charity and joy, founded on reciprocity, trust-worthiness and stable commitment. In the writings of Richard of St Victor, developing the thoughts of Cicero, it is this same-sex partnership which offers an understanding of the Trinity. Marilyn Adams has extensively considered these ideas in her article 'Trinitarian Friendship: Same-gender models of godly love in Richard of St Victor and Aelred of Rievaulx'.[8]

That is not to say that ethics can be simply reduced to statements about Love justifying all. The Bible presents us with a people striving to be faithful to a God who has brought them into a new place. But faithfulness to their tra-dition does not oblige us to believe that their detailed working out of themes about sexuality and the role of the sexes is the right way in the light of modern knowledge to respond to the God of incarnation and of resurrection. A major and continuing strand in their tradition, and in the teaching of Jesus, is that faithlessness was most often man-ifested by failing to grasp God's new thing when it came. Throughout history it has been a characteristic of religious institutions that they have had huge difficulty in embrac-ing change, because they have claimed such exclusive asso-ciation of God with the views they hold. The running conflict between Jesus and the religious establishment of his day is only one illustration of this abiding tendency.

The debate intensifies

Notwithstanding all the calls for dialogue, the year 2003 saw the debate grow more intense: three causes were the nomination (subsequently declined) of Canon Jeffrey John to be Bishop of Reading and, across the Atlantic, the conse-cration of Canon Gene Robinson as Bishop of New Hampshire and the beginning of same-sex blessings in the Canadian diocese of New Westminster. The Bishop of St Edmundsbury and Ipswich in the presidential address to his diocesan synod in November 2003 said of the wide-spread dismay:

It was not simply a matter of people being for or against. It was more complex than that, and in learning how we handle our differences, we need to understand something of that complexity, otherwise the debate just becomes a fracas in the playground and in the end it is the loudest voices which tend to prevail.

For those inclined to think the crisis rather over-stated, the bishop said he had talked with a number of gay people, particularly young ones, who know that if they raise any question about their sexuality they will either be asked to leave their church or it will be made too difficult to stay.

These are not isolated instances, there are many people who find themselves in this situation – one letter alone was signed by eighteen young gay people who are struggling to hold on to their church membership despite the odds.

The clerical dilemma

The bishops in *Issues in Human Sexuality*[9] made a distinction between lay homophiles (the term preferred in that report), whose loving, faithful and intentionally lifelong partnerships they could not commend (though they would not reject those who sincerely believed that God called them to such partnerships), and homophile clergy whose pastoral responsibilities, the bishops argued, barred them from any sexually active homophile relationships, however committed and long-term in intention. The film *Priest* in the mid-1990s brought to many people with particular poignancy the agony of homosexuals in the Roman Catholic priesthood and, by extension, in the Church of England.

Some Issues[10] tries to respond to the criticism that it is difficult for congregations to become 'places of open acceptance and friendship for homophiles' (as encouraged in *Issues*) if there are no openly gay and lesbian clergy to be role models of loving and faithful partnership. First, it argues that such role models would contradict the Church's traditional teaching on marriage and abstinence; second, it adopts the arguments that social factors have been highly influential in causing young people at an age

when easily led mistakenly to claim a homosexual identity
not properly theirs; were there to be clergy role models,
that temptation might be even greater. Many would dispute that social factors can draw young people to assume a
homosexual identity which is not theirs.

Some Issues (even while purporting to offer itself as a
guide for debate) argues that clergy must be exemplary in
their sexual conduct and that it is scandalous if they are
not. Such an argument is circular, or contradictory, in
claiming willingness to listen to the experience of gay partners, yet ruling out the possibility that clergy in gay relationships have experience to offer, indicating that there is
something intrinsically deficient which makes clergy same-
sex relationships an inappropriate model, and therefore
discouraging both congregational acceptance and the risky
frankness of discussion by lay people involved in same-sex
partnerships. And how are lay people whose partners are
clergy to respond?

The issue of bisexuality is one which *Some Issues* slides
over quickly.[11] It relates it largely to promiscuity and
against a heterosexual standard. It fails to consider clergy
who, within the oppressive atmosphere of secrecy, have
married and seek to maintain their marriage vows and
family life, yet are aware that their nature is substantially
homosexual and not to be expressed. Such situations are
not infrequently the stuff of tragedy.

Do these arguments go to the root of Christian polity?
Not all heterosexual clergy are able to maintain lifelong
faithfulness, and the Church now has provision for resum-
ing ministry when divorce and remarriage have occurred,
even in some circumstances when there has been scandal.
And whether the Church acknowledges it or not, there
have been for many years homosexual clergy in committed
faithful partnerships. The flaw in the argument has been
the pressure for these to remain clandestine, so subjecting
them to unnatural pressure and making such partnerships
less likely to survive. Only of homosexual clergy does the
Church of England require celibacy. This is patronising in
itself, unrealistic in terms of what is actually the case, limiting in terms of theological understanding, and divisive in
terms of the mutuality of clergy and laity within the total

Body of Christ. While this remains so, it is less easy for congregations to be 'places of acceptance and friendship' for lay homophiles, as congregations are encouraged to be by the bishops in *Some Issues*, and yet there are many congregations which still manage to be that.

The being of a priest

Stronger arguments still may be drawn from the nature of priesthood. In the debate on the ordination of women, it came to be seen as important that the priest at the altar is representative both of God and of humanity. Limiting the priesthood to men gave an inadequate picture of God engaged in Eucharist as only masculine. One form of the argument developed by those opposed to women priests claimed that the priest in the Eucharist represented God whose (masculine) nature was to initiate, while the Church in feminine mode was passively to respond. Female priests would confuse that imagery. Sexuality was seen by that school of thought as integral to the argument, but it was a sexuality streamlined along a strict demarcation. Where were the 'feminine' qualities of God, the passive respondent, who on the Cross and in the Eucharist lets humans take initiative? Such a stark division between masculine and feminine, between initiator and passive respondent, was not a true description then, nor is it now. Each of us in our complex sexuality reflects the glory and the mystery of God.

Symbols are polyvalent. They overlap and interchange and do not have rigid boundaries. One gender can represent all humanity. Jesus did upon the Cross. But the richness of the point about humanity comes across more strongly when different genders at various times take that role, with their complex identities. Then we have a better picture of the 'all' that is being represented.

No one is quite like another. The essential fact of Jesus was not that he was male, but that he was a person, an individual with his own sexuality, no less complex than any other human being. Certainly, as a recent book[12] puts it 'Maleness cannot damage, or limit, humanness. If that were so, the incarnation would not be real. The whole of

17

humanity can be equally represented by a male or a female.' But what is remarkable is not the maleness or the femaleness, but that an individual, any one individual in all his or her varied circumstances, may represent the whole of humanity. Not only humanity. He or she may represent God.

The married male priest who has made love with his wife represents God at the altar as much as does the celibate priest who is wholly abstinent. So does the female priest who has made love with her husband. Why should the homosexual priest who from a committed relationship draws the experience of intimacy and affection, of fidelity and generosity, of surrender and acceptance, be any less a priest? Any less representative of God's initiative, any less representative of God's passion and passivity?

Spiritual and sacramental

We are far from understanding the relationship between sexuality and spirituality, but there seems some evidence that many homosexual priests have particularly creative spiritual gifts from which the Church has gained. As Archbishop Rowan Williams has written, in a passage quoted in *Some Issues*:

> [Because] Jesus is himself the first and greatest sacrament, and he creates the possibility of things and persons, acts and places, being in some way sacramental in the light of what he has done.
>
> Now, if my life can communicate the 'meanings' of God, this must mean that my sexuality too can be sacramental; it can speak of mercy, faithfulness, transfiguration and hope. Whatever the temptation, we are not to give up on this aspect of ourselves, as if it couldn't speak of God. For all the danger and complexity, it isn't outside the sacramental potential given us in Christ.[13]

The God whom priests represent at the altar is the God of Trinity, a God of diversity and difference. Each human being in their own difference reflects the glory of God seen quite like that in no one else. The homosexual and the heterosexual alike reflect the glory of God, as the bishops acknowledged in *Issues* in 1991. But that true

18

humanity does not exist in vertical relationship with God alone; the God of Trinity who in Christ brings us into relationship with the Godhead calls us each to reflect that relationship in a relationship with other people. As the Genesis story tells us, it is not good for us to be alone; married or celibate, heterosexual or homosexual, we need to find ways of expressing in friendship and charity the open, non-exclusive, expanding aspect of God's love.

If sexuality lies behind the human quest for completeness, the attraction to others and the desire for intimate physical contact, a distinction may still be drawn between touching and embracing, and the genital contact which is the focus of so much traditional sexual legislation. Yet it is in that search for the other in whom the one finds completion that the homosexual partnership, like the heterosexual partnership, would claim that love can be at its most full and generous.

Nature and norm

The traditional view of homosexuality is that it is unnatural. It would be more accurate to say that it is abnormal. It is natural in that it occurs in nature, in the natural state, and not only in human beings. There is some evidence that it is a widespread condition in nature. It is, however, abnormal in the sense that it is not the statistical norm. Being not the norm does not make it colloquially abnormal. In the diversity of creation that which is not the norm has its place alongside that which is more normal. The norm is the coming together of man and wife in a family unit for the procreation and upbringing of children. Robert Adams' essay looks in greater detail at the relationship between norm and nature.

Alongside these family units society has need of a range of people whose temperament and circumstances fit them for other creative tasks. Many of these may be single, many may be homosexual in inclination; the argument that they do not conform to the norm is not sufficient to rule out their finding physical expression of their love. The homosexual priest at the altar would be no less expressive of the range of humanity than his or her heterosexual brother or sister.

And now

Although published as a discussion document, *Issues* rapidly acquired the status of official policy which bishops became expected to acknowledge (under pressure from media and sections of the Church). While *Some Issues* states that, 'it does not seek to change the position of the House of Bishops from the one established' in *Issues*, that position remains one to which discussion is invited and expected. The use of the word 'debate' is interesting. As *Some Issues* says, the resolution of the 1998 Lambeth Conference 'remains the nearest thing there is to an official statement by the Anglican Communion on the subject, though it needs to be remembered that resolutions of the Lambeth Conference have not been seen as binding upon the Anglican Communion'.[14] There is much still to be discussed, and other chapters in this book will explore this from a range of angles which have not so far been fully brought into the debate.

Notes

1 *Some Issues in Human Sexuality: A guide to the debate* (Church House Publishing, 2003).
2 *Christian Action Journal* (Autumn 1979), p.15.
3 Alec Vidler (ed.), *Soundings: Essays concerning Christian understanding* (Cambridge University Press, 1964).
4 John Saxbee (now Bishop of Lincoln), *Liberal Evangelism: A flexible approach to the decade* (SPCK, 1994).
5 Keith Ward, *God: A guide for the perplexed* (OneWorld, 2002), p.78.
6 A. M. Ramsey, *Introducing the Christian Faith* (SCM, 1961), p.39.
7 Keith Ward, *God*, p.71.
8 Marilyn McCord Adams, 'Trinitarian Friendship: Same-gender models of godly love in Richard of St Victor and Aelred of Rievaulx', Chapter 29 in *Theology and Sexuality*, ed. by Eugene F. Rogers, Jr (Oxford: Blackwell, 1988), pp.322-40.
9 *Issues in Human Sexuality* (Church House Publishing, 1991).
10 *Some Issues in Human Sexuality*.
11 ibid. pp.282-4.
12 Jonathan Baker (ed.), *Consecrated Women: Women bishops – a Catholic and Evangelical response* (Canterbury Press, 2004).

13 *Some Issues in Human Sexuality*, p.111.
14 ibid. p.31.

2 'The letter killeth, but the Spirit giveth life': Christian biblical interpretation

Christopher Rowland

This is an essay on the Bible and its place in Christian discipleship. It is not about the explanation of the details of those texts which have been at the heart of the controversy about homosexuality in the Church. Its main focus is on how it is that Christians should approach what have come to be seen as authoritative texts in the light of the prime Christian commitment to follow Christ and, to quote Paul's words, 'to be found in him' (Philippians 3:9). While it appeals to the information found in the New Testament, it does so in order to question whether Christians of this or any generation should approach scriptural texts as if their contents should be prescriptive. The New Testament writings themselves point us to a form of Christian commitment which bids us look to texts from the past never as the prime source of understanding of the divine will. That is Christ through the Spirit pointing and guiding the Church. In this the Scriptures may be the vehicle of the divine Spirit, but Christ is never exclusively bound to them. So, whether or not Paul's words in Romans 1 and 1 Corinthians 6 exclude practising homosexuals from the Christian community is not the concern of this essay. Rather, its task is to ask the basic question: what is the role of the Bible in enabling those who claim to be followers of Jesus Christ to discern what it means to be true to their calling?

There is a widespread conviction, with a long history in Christian theology and rooted in the Bible itself, that the prime responsibility of a Christian is to find Christ outside, rather than primarily inside, the pages of Scripture.[1] Thus

the influential twentieth-century systematic theologian
Karl Barth wrote:

> Why and in what respect does the biblical witness have author-
> ity? Because, and in the fact that, he claims no authority for
> himself, that his witness amounts to letting that other be itself
> its own authority. We thus do the Bible poor and unwelcome
> honour if we equate it directly with the other, with revelation
> itself.[2]

Elsewhere, Barth is more outspoken still in describing the
consequences of such an equation:

> We have to resist and reject the seventeenth-century doctrine of
> inspiration as false doctrine . . . The Bible was now grounded
> upon itself, apart from the mystery of Christ and the Holy
> Spirit. It became a 'paper Pope', and, unlike the Pope in Rome
> it was wholly given up into the hands of interpreters. It was no
> longer a free and spiritual force but an instrument of human
> power.[3]

Barth's position has its analogies with some of the radical
writers of the time of the Reformation, whose views on the
Bible were often at odds with the mainstream writers of
the Reformation. Hans Denck died of plague in his late
twenties, in 1527. He was what would come to be called an
Anabaptist, having undergone re-baptism as a sign of his
own commitment to Christ and his move to a new way of
life, one in which violence was abhorred and attentiveness
to the law of God written on the heart was the norm for
Christian living. To many Anglicans, Anabaptism spells the
negative effects of sectarianism, but some of the earliest
Anabaptists were remarkable Christian humanists and
their writings deserve to be more widely known. Foremost
among these is Hans Denck. What is relevant for our contemporary discussions is the priority given to obedience to
Christ, the divine Word, over against the words in the
pages of Scripture. What Denck points us to is that discerning the divine will is less about minute textual exegesis and more about discernment, in which Christians
must be informed by a range of insights, not only the
insights of Scripture and tradition, but also by the way
in which God meets them in everyday life, especially in

human relationships, thereby enabling themselves to be open to a God who calls them to new life and ways of living which seek to be in continuity with the way of Christ. Christianity is therefore not a religion which appeals solely to the past.

In a piece published shortly after his death, Denck wrote:

> Holy Scripture I hold above all human treasure but not as high as the Word of God that is living, powerful and eternal – unattached and free of all elements of this world; for since it is God himself, it is Spirit and not letter, written without pen or paper so that it can never be eradicated . . . Therefore, salvation is not bound to Scripture however useful and good it might be in furthering it.[4]

Scripture, therefore, may bear witness to the Word which became flesh, Jesus Christ, and the indwelling divine Word, who comes again and again, encouraging and challenging men and women. Its authority is dependent upon the confirmation of the experience from within. It is the inner experience of God present in all people which is fundamental, even though they may not recognise it. For Denck, therefore, much as in the Epistle of James 2 and 1 John 4:7-21, religion is the transformation of the individual and the good deeds which are the result.

The need to discern the call of God in everyday human experience has its modern analogy in the method of liberation theology. Liberation theology is a form of theology, in which experience and the insight of social context are given a prime place. God does not come from outside the situation but is to be found there as much as in the tradition itself, as the poignant words of the Son of Man in the story of the last judgement in Matthew 25:31-45 indicate: 'inasmuch as you have done it to one of the least of these you have done it to me'. The quest for God starts with the quest for love of brothers and sisters and moves to the love of God, and back again from the love of God to love of one's brothers and one's sisters, from the quest amidst the struggle for human justice to God's justice and holiness. Theology, therefore, involves an understanding of faith from a position within real solidarity with all suffering and exploited people. Theology is not worked out in isolation from the pressing human realities, for in those realities the Spirit of God speaks to people and beckons them to find the way of God. It is theology geared to action. Christ is to be found outside, as well as inside the lives of Christian communities, pointing to new ways of following, and beckoning to people to be part of that new life.

Obviously the position of Barth, and Denck before him, is not without difficulties. If we seek to know what Christ was like and his character, then the Scriptures are the obvious place to go. Nevertheless, from the very start of Christian history mere appeal to 'what the Bible says' was never deemed to be an adequate ground for the Christian life. As Christianity sought to offer a message for those outside the bounds of Judaism, it rapidly became necessary to show how Christ might have been involved in the culture of society. Early Christian writers did this by stressing that the divine Word was already active in the lives of men and women centuries before, without their ever being part of the people of God. The opening of the Gospel of John, which speaks of the true light enlightening every one coming into the world, broadened the horizons of the activity of Christ beyond the records of Jesus' life in the pages of the gospel.

When seeking to discern what may be of God and what not, early Christian writers used a complex mix of appeal to tradition, to recognised bearers of the way, and to what they termed 'a rule of faith', a simple formula, probably the forerunner of the Christian creeds, which offered a benchmark for those who would select true teaching from false. Such a mix did not solely involve a simple appeal to the past, something which from the very start had never been at the heart of Christianity (whose origins lay in a radically new reading of received wisdom, claiming a degree of continuity with them but never allowing what had been written in the past to determine what God's Spirit was calling people to in the present). It is here that the Christian conviction that the Spirit who, among other things, opens up the meaning of the letters of Scripture to the eye of faith, comes into play (cf. 2 Corinthians 3:6).

In discerning what the Spirit is now saying to the churches, the words and character of Jesus have always remained fundamental for Christian living, and to this extent the Scriptures are a necessary component in providing the way of attending to the words of the Word become flesh. This is the message of Jesus to his disciples in the Gospel of John. The divine spirit leads the disciples into all truth. There is new revelation to be expected (John 16:13), but any revelation is in continuity with what Jesus has said. The Spirit only takes what is of Jesus and makes that known to the disciples. There is, therefore, both a retrospective and prospective action of the Spirit: looking back to Jesus and expecting new insights from the divine Spirit. There is nothing here about the words of the Bible as a whole. The words of Jesus, yes – and appeal also to the character of the one who, according to the Gospel of John, left his disciples one commandment only, 'that you love one another as I have loved you' (John 13:34). It is not just words, therefore. It is the Word become flesh. In the New Testament, the verb from which we get the word 'exegesis' or interpretation, what it is we do when we try and make sense of the words in the Bible, is found in the New Testament in John 1:18, where Christ is described as one who explains or offers an 'exegesis' of the unseen God. Similarly, in Hebrews 1:1 the writer compares God's words spoken through the prophets of the past with the decisive word which God has spoken by his Son. John 1:18 and Hebrews 1:1-4 point in the direction of discerning the will of God beyond verbal paraphrase or grammatical explanation, and suggest that practical demonstration of meaning in the living out of the meaning of the biblical words, is as, if not more, important.

That is what we find with Paul. He was capable, on occasion (e.g. 1 Corinthians 7:10 and 11:23), of appealing to the words of Jesus, in order to remind those who would concentrate solely on the present that their faith had to keep in touch with their origins rooted in what Jesus had said and done. Nevertheless, such an appeal is complemented, if not transcended, by the living witness to Christ in persons who seek to live in conformity with Christ. That is more important than obedience to the words from the past.

Less than twenty years after the death of Jesus, Jews and pagans in a city in Syria were eating together on a regular basis. Some Jews in that context relaxed the rules which had hitherto maintained their identity. Perhaps there was a history of such commensality among Jews in Antioch as members of a minority culture sought to maintain social intercourse with men and women who did not share their faith. Whatever may have been the antecedents, in Antioch in the 40s CE, experience of God, and of others who claimed to be followers of Jesus, led those men and women to new patterns of behaviour which were at odds with what most of their co-religionists practised. Paul describes the behaviour of those Christians in Antioch in his Letter to the Galatians, when he stood up in defence of them to his fellow church leaders, including Peter, who had suddenly got cold feet about their participation in this kind of table-fellowship. Not surprisingly such activity caused scandals to more conservative elements in the church. Representations were sent from the churches in Jerusalem asking Paul, and these newly established communities, to desist from what might have appeared to some people 'unscriptural' behaviour. It is clear from the passion with which Paul writes in his letter that standing up to those who did not want to rock the boat was crucial for him. There was something important about the Gospel practice which was in danger of being sacrificed by the attempt to try to be in continuity with the past. Paul had little or no basis in Scripture for the kind of common table that he was supporting, in which Jews and pagans ate their meals together. Nevertheless, his decision to support and encourage this kind of mixed dining and shared fellowship was absolutely central to what he understood his faith to be about. In his letter to the Corinthians (chapter 11), he reproaches those Christians in Corinth who would cause division, this time on class lines rather than on ethnic lines, and stresses the unity of the community in the one Spirit (1 Corinthians 12:13).

In this dispute, and in much of Paul's discussions about the Bible, Paul's opponents had all the best arguments, for they had precedent and Scripture on their side. Take the case of Abraham. Paul picks on Abraham's 'justification by faith' in Genesis 15:6 as an example of the way in which God justifies the ungodly without obedience to the Law. What he omits, however, is that just two chapters later, the

Bible mentions that God instructed Abraham to circumcise himself and his son, Ishmael (Genesis 17:11-14, 23-4). Paul, the budding rabbi, must have been aware of this. Though he had some grounds in the Scriptures, they were nothing like as strong as his opponents' scriptural backing. Nevertheless, despite this, Paul was persuaded that the experience of God of those pagans, who had converted to Christ, corresponded to what he, and other Jewish Christians, had experienced, and they enjoyed the authentic mark of God's presence, without resort to the preservation of ancestral customs. What mattered most was that something which was in continuity with Christ was being done in their midst, not that the past was being preserved. Jews and pagans who followed Christ could leave behind fundamentals of the ancestral Scriptures and live in different kinds of communities, with different norms of behaviour, based on conformity to Christ, which still managed to exhibit the fundamentals of love of God and neighbour, whatever they ate. In so doing they left Judaism behind, however much the Christians might have liked to have thought that what they were doing was in continuity with Jewish tradition.

There is something similar going on in the story which is told about Peter's journey to Cornelius in the Acts of the Apostles. The pious Jew was persuaded to different attitudes to non-Jews and changed behaviour as a result of his ecstatic experience, when he saw the sheet descending from heaven, full of unclean animals. The instruction in his vision to 'sacrifice and eat' cut across the very heart of his ancestral laws which, the Acts story tells us, Peter had kept. Yet this experience offered an endorsement of his proclamation to Cornelius. This was confirmed by the witness of the conversion of the Roman centurion Cornelius, without first converting to Judaism. Peter, we are told, believed that the same God was at work in these pagan converts as had been at work in the first Christians. So he asserts 'God gave the pagans the same gift as us when we believed, who was I to hinder God?' (Acts 11:17).

What both Peter and Paul were doing was relativising the place of Scripture and tradition in the light of the present experience of the Spirit, who will 'guide them into all truth' (John 16:13); in Paul's case of the new habits of life in the Antioch community, in Peter's case an extraordinary visionary experience then confirmed by the dramatic conversion of a pagan soldier. Scripture had to be viewed afresh, with its meaning determined by the experience of the love of Christ and the obvious marks of God's presence in the lives of those who, according to the law, should be outsiders.

In doing this, they laid down an approach to their ancestral Scriptures which should be central to Christianity. Christianity has never been a religion of the book. However comforting appeal to precedent or a written text might be, there is in Christianity's own foundation texts the story of a movement which, when it came to the crunch, was prepared to sit loose to ancestral custom and to prefer patterns of life which seemed to be in conformity with something fundamental to the Christ they experienced. Thanks to Paul, Christianity has never ever been a religion that used the Bible as if it were a law code. In his Second Letter to the Corinthians, Paul writes: 'the letter kills, the Spirit gives life.' By this he meant that engaging with Scripture is to try to get at what the Bible might point to about conformity to Christ rather than be preoccupied with what its literal demands are. Paul pioneered an approach to the Bible of his own day (what Christians would now call the Old Testament), therefore, which should also apply to those of us who now look back on his words preserved in the Scripture which we now call the New Testament. We should not be concentrating on the letter of Paul's words, but trying to get at the underlying point of his words, to discern how they might help us, at a different time and place, to be imitators of Christ. That is what Paul's words suggest: not to be slavish followers of his words.

Basing one's attitudes towards gay and lesbian people merely on two verses from Romans and 1 Corinthians runs the risk of ending up treating the Bible as law code. Instead we need to be aware that Christ, who is alive and active in the world, may be calling men and women to new adventures in the life of faith. This will depend not on the letter of the text, but on using the Bible as part of the complex

29

way of discerning what the divine Spirit is now saying to the churches. The appeal to 'what the Bible says' is what Paul so emphatically opposes, for he would point us to what a loving God is doing in transforming and enabling lives in the present through the Spirit.

Theologically, this is the most important matter discussed in this article. Too often Christians have ended up functioning as if they did not have a doctrine of the Spirit, or, if they have, somehow the voice of the Spirit is identified with the text of Scripture or what Christians have said in the past (more accurately, what the majority, and most influential, Christian voices have said). To take seriously the fact that 'the letter killeth, but the Spirit giveth life' (2 Corinthians 3:6) means quite simply that God's Spirit may be saying a new thing and not merely supporting what Christians have always said. When writing to the Corinthians, Paul stressed how important it was to enable the Spirit to speak and inform the life of the Christian community. That could never be identified with the words of Scripture, and, as he reminded the Corinthians in 1 Corinthians 2:10-16, there is a profound interaction between the human and divine spirit as the search goes on for discernment of the way of discipleship. Of course, the ability of humans to get things wrong cannot be gainsaid, nor should this essay be seen as subscribing to the naïve view that modern people are somehow more enlightened. We should attend to what our ancestors in the faith have said (all of them, including Hans Denck and those whose voices are ignored, not just those the mainstream churches choose to hear, and who are regarded as the mainstays of tradition). The risk of making a mistake should not short-circuit the patient quest to be attentive to the Spirit. One of the disasters for Christianity, from the first century to today, is the ease with which we have pressed the panic button in the face of deep disagreement, anathematised dissent and behaved in ways which are in flagrant contradiction to the primacy of charity, 'the very bond of peace and of all virtues', as the Collect puts it. Because we may err in our judgements of what the Spirit is saying to us neither absolves us of the difficult task of discernment, a collective enterprise if ever there was one, nor faces up to the recognition of the possibility that Christians in the past may have erred. They did about slavery and the role of women – to take two examples. It is at least a question worth asking that they may also have done so in relation to homosexual relationships. How one goes about maximising participation in decision-making in community, Paul spends a considerable amount of effort seeking to elucidate in 1 Corinthians. In 1 Corinthians 14, for example, he sets out a pattern of communal responsiveness to the Spirit, in which the different gifts contribute to the building-up of the whole community. This process has to take place before understanding can come. The ethos for this to take place is absence of boasting and self-assertiveness, as well as the spiritual narcissism in which the Corinthian community abounds. No one has the right to boast, and all need to be attentive to the other, so that the love about which Paul writes in 1 Corinthians 13 can abound, as the community, in faith and hope, seeks to move towards that time when God will be all in all.

The debate about homosexuality is a debate about the nature of the Christian religion. In this article I have challenged the idea that Christianity is a religion of the book. Christianity did not start like that, and to seek to be true to the method of Paul as he interprets Scripture is to recognise that what is central in the life of Christians is obedience to the divine Spirit in our own time. Three overlapping interpretative approaches are going on in this article. The first reflects the issue posed by Hans Denck that Christ is to be found not solely in the words of Scripture, but in the imprint of God's word upon human lives and hearts, as well as in the Christian believers and in the Church. Jesus in John's gospel speaks of the Spirit coming to convict the world of sin, justice and judgement. That activity goes on, irrespective of the Church's ability to understand and respond adequately. The Holy Spirit, poured out on all flesh, is active and it is in co-operation with the action of the Spirit that all are called to be responsive.

The second approach has been a reading of the biblical text in the light of what I, as a modern interpreter, consider to be its essential subject matter. I have focused on particular themes to interpret the whole of the Pauline letters, such as the unity of Jew and Gentile in Christ, the importance of mutual love, and the concern for building up rather than strife. That judgement, of course, is contestable, and is a contribution to an ongoing debate among people who deeply disagree about a range of issues. Between the accounts of the pluralist community of Corinth, with its various gifted individuals and the variety of its congregational life in 1 Corinthians 12 and 14, there stands Paul's lyrical description of love in 1 Corinthians 13 and its centrality for Christian communities who still await perfection. It is this fundamental subject matter which is the criterion, the criterion of love and mutual acceptance, by which other less prominent pieces, such as the occasional reference to homosexuality, is to be judged.

Finally, I have sought to articulate a response in the light of deeply held convictions by contemporary Christians, with which I wholeheartedly agree, that they are being faithful to Jesus Christ in being in same-sex relationships. In so doing, I have made use of a method which comes from liberation theology. In this the contemporary engagement with the text in our particular context and in the light of our social issues and struggle to be obedient to Christ is a way of opening up the meaning of Scripture. The relationship between the biblical texts as a witness to the struggles of Christians in their context to pursue the way of Jesus can in turn then throw light on our present debates. As such there is interplay between present and past, so that our present decisions are open to the possibility of critical scrutiny, though not judgement, from the insights of those who have gone before us.

The living witness to Christ in the lives of those who seek to live in conformity with Christ is more important than obedience to the words from the past, even those of Jesus, which Paul respectfully ignored in pursing what he thought was appropriate in his own life, as 1 Corinthians 9:14-15 indicates. This is an important passage and reminds us that Paul did not believe that simple appeal to what had been passed on, even the words of the Lord, should prevent Christians seeking to be attentive to what the Spirit was saying to the churches, here and now. He appeals to the Corinthians to be 'imitators of me as I am of Christ' (1

Corinthians 11:1). So, lives lived in different times and places, which exemplify the pattern of Christ, are what are most important. These do not merely imitate what Jesus did in Galilee and Jerusalem. Few Christians would want to practise exorcisms as Jesus did, according to the gospels, even if we too would be wanting to engage with the powers of evil, whether personal or social, in our own way and for our own time. What we are struggling to understand and embody are the contours of the *character* of Christ, as Philippians 2:6-11 indicates. We cannot know what this is just by appealing to Scripture or tradition though we will want to be aware of it. What we shall need to do is share experiences of seeking to live life in service to Christ, recognise our differences, and *together* be in the quest of truth, rather than assuming that we know what this is. After all, it is Christ alone who is that truth and, at most, Scripture may bear witness to that truth. We can (and should) go to the New Testament, primarily the gospels, as part of the process of discerning what it is that the Spirit points us to.

How the stories about Jesus Christ impact on us in our time and place is the result of our openness to the stories and words in the gospels and our mutual appropriation of them as we seek to live lives of faith. To be transformed into the likeness of Christ is a process of growth and not just the application of clear-cut rules. It involves mutual edification and criticism, which ultimately depends on owning and accepting difference and diversity in the community which is journeying together. We may find this in seeking to live with each other, accepting our differences. In so doing we shall be doing little that is different from what Christians have always done. Take the issue of peace and war. No one would deny that the words and example of Jesus as found in the gospels are unequivocal on the matter. Today, however, Christians are found deeply divided between those who accept the 'Just War' and those who remain pacifists. In dealing with this they have not stopped talking with one another, or been anathematising those with whom they disagree. There will be deeply held convictions on both sides. We shall not resolve the differences this side of the Last Judgement. That is the time to leave the issue of judgement and not to indulge in anathemas on those with whom we disagree. Paul's advice is worth heeding: 'Why do you pass judgement on your brother or sister? Or you, why do you despise your brother or sister? For we will stand before the judgement seat of God' (Romans 14:10).

On the Damascus road, Saul's world was turned upside down. He encountered Christ in the outsiders, the heretics, the misfits and aliens, the very people whom he had been commissioned to seek out and to round up. It was this experience that transformed Paul's life. Such a turn around was not the result of minute attention to text and precedent. The era of Paul and his founding of the Early Church was a time of experimentation as to what it meant to be God's people. As such, it may be particularly apposite for our time. Like Paul and his communities, the simple appeal to Scripture and tradition may have to be questioned as we seek to discern the call of the divine Word, who bids us recognise that the gifts of God are at work in gay and lesbian Christians, and in their loving, committed relationships, as in heterosexual relationships. Furthermore, the God who called Paul to explore new patterns of relationship is at work in committed same-sex relationships, and this tells us something of the love of the divine Spirit who seeks to guide us into all truth, which is the goal we seek. Meanwhile, we see in a glass darkly (1 Corinthians 13:12) and in conformity with Christ practise love one towards another, as, together, we seek to follow Jesus Christ who is the truth and who will reveal that truth when we stand before him on the Last Day.

For further reading

John Barton, *People of the Book? The Authority of the Bible in Christianity* (London: SPCK, 1988). This wonderful little book makes a very similar case for the primacy of Christian devotion to Christ rather than Scripture and does so with great learning and in a very accessible fashion.

Stuart Murray, *Biblical Interpretation in the Anabaptist Tradition* (Kitchener, Ontario: Pandora, 2000), offers a concise introduction to the distinctive elements of early Anabaptist scriptural interpretation.

Notes

1 We can see a position similar to this enunciated in the Windsor Report of 2004 paragraphs 54-5: 'When Jesus speaks of "all authority in heaven and earth" (Matthew 28:18), he declares that this authority is given, not to the books that his followers will write, but to himself. Jesus, the living Word, is the one to whom the written Word bears witness as God's ultimate and personal self-expression. The New Testament is full of similar ascriptions of authority to the Father, to Jesus Christ, and to the Holy Spirit. Thus the phrase "the authority of scripture", if it is to be based on what scripture itself says, must be regarded as a shorthand, and a potentially misleading one at that, for the longer and more complex notion of "the authority of the triune God, *exercised through* scripture" . . . If the notion of scriptural authority is itself to be rooted in scripture, and to be consonant with the central truths confessed by Christians from the earliest days, it must be seen that the purpose of scripture is not simply to supply true information, nor just to prescribe in matters of belief and conduct, nor merely to act as a court of appeal, but to be part of the dynamic life of the Spirit through which God the Father is making the victory which was won by Jesus' death and resurrection operative within the world and in and through human beings. Scripture is thus part of the means by which God directs the Church in its mission, energises it for that task, and shapes and unites it so that it may be both equipped for this work and itself part of the message.'

2 Karl Barth, *Church Dogmatics: The doctrine of the word of God. Volume 1* (Edinburgh: T & T Clark, 1975), pp.125-6.

3 ibid. p.525.

4 *Recantation* 1, translation from Clarence Bauman, *The Spiritual Legacy of Hans Denck: Interpretation and translation of key texts* (Leiden: Brill, 1991), p.251.

© 2005 Christopher Rowland

3 Sexuality without taboos

Marilyn McCord Adams

Speaking into the winds of change

We human beings are embodied persons. Theologically, our sexuality is a powerful creative force at the core of our personalities and as such is one way in which we image God. Psychologically, healthy human functioning requires our sexuality not to be split off or compartmentalised, but integrated into our personalities as a whole. Politically, even in a liberal society, sexual expression cannot be entirely privatised. Because of its power to bind and to bond, to divide and destroy, because of its reproductive potential and its role in propagating and preserving the human race, sexual practices are shot through with social implications.

Human societies have invented a variety of institutions to house human sexual expression. The Bible itself spans a roughly 2,000-year period, and reflects different institutions at different times in a variety of cultural situations. Socially and legally, there is no single institution of 'biblical marriage'. What it was to be married varied considerably in patriarchal Bedouin tribes (Abraham to Sarah, Jacob to Rachel and Leah), in early monarchical times (David and Solomon with their harems) and in imperial Rome (Peter to his wife). In the background of the Bible's stories are both cultural clashes and controversial syncretism between the sexual institutions of Israel and its neighbours (e.g., over temple prostitution in Canaanite religion and nudity in the athletic gymnasiums of Antiochus Epiphanes). Similar dramas are played out today in conflicts between traditionalist and 'westernising' or 'modernising' parties in Islamic countries: e.g., whether marriages are arranged by families, whether women wear the veil, what sorts of rights women have vis a vis their husbands and children. Late nineteenth- and early-twentieth-century anthropologists startled Europe and America by charting sharply contrasting patterns of kinship and gender roles in societies around the world.

Social institutions – including those that house and manage sexual relations and gender roles – change over time, due in no small part to economic and demographic factors (e.g., polygamy drops out when it becomes too expensive and when more children are an economic burden rather than a welcome increase in the labour force). While challenges may be abrupt, the evolution of old institutions into new ones is a gradual process that takes at least decades to settle down. The precise shape of wholesome and workable institutions depends on many factors that are difficult to anticipate and account for and impossible to control. To some extent, we see what we have been and what we are, but it does not yet appear what we shall be. Likewise, the full implications of the changes we initiate are impossible to map out in advance.

Where sexual mores and gender roles are concerned, we find ourselves in a period of social change. At least since the sixties, consensus around sex and gender institutions has been eroding along numerous parameters: the indissolubility of marriage (except for grave fault); the impossibility of the remarriage of divorced persons; the prohibition of genital sexual activity outside marriage; the ideal of virginity before marriage; the ban against cohabitation without benefit of clergy; the criminal status of homosexual activity; and the notion that a woman's place is in the home. This ungluing of consensus spans the age spectrum: not only is sexual activity among teenagers taken for granted, extra-marital cohabitation is countenanced and common among consenting adults, whether young, middle-aged or senior citizens. Young couples, some from divorced homes, and middle-aged pairs, perhaps with bad marriages in their pasts, want to 'try it out' to see whether it will work before they tie the knot. Senior citizens do not want to compromise their children's inheritance by late-in-life remarriage. Practices are still in flux. Some legal changes have occurred – with provisions for divorce and domestic partnerships and the decriminalising of homosexuality and abortion. But many ideas are in the air; many lifestyle experiments are still in progress. As yet, there is no new consensus around sex and gender institutions. On the contrary, it is common for polemicists to speak of ongoing 'cultural wars'. Change is happening whether we like it or not. The question is how the Church can make a constructive contribution to the process.

The Church has always seen itself as called to give normative guidance where sexual practices are concerned, but the kind of guidance relevant and possible is different in times of social transition from what is called for when new equilibria have been reached. In the past, the Church has risen to the occasion and accepted the price of a certain amount of trial and error and thinking on its feet. Unexpected Gentile conversions pressed St Paul to give advice about eating meat sacrificed to idols, about staying married to unbelieving partners, about the wisdom of celibacy and sexual abstinence when the end-time seems near. After several hundred years of unmarried clergy, Protestant reformers found themselves re-examining the goods of marriage, even toying with bigamy as a response to infertile spouses or partners with impaired sexual performance. Nor does the Church stand above the fray and view the struggle *sub specie aeternitatis*. Institutionally, the Church is shaped by the cultures it shapes and to which it speaks. Humanly, it has neither foreknowledge nor power to control the outcome. For the Church, the challenge is how to point itself and the wider society towards a deep-structure reintegration of institutions that will enable human sexual practice to proclaim Good News in our contemporary world, to advertise fresh and wholesome meanings for human life and divine–human relations. To exercise good and godly discernment in the midst of change, it may help to be alert to different layers and modalities of social entrenchment.

Taboos versus institutions

Institutions as 'explicit order'

Human sanity and survival require us to impose some sort of order on the world that makes it seem stable and predictable. Science does this at the *natural* level. At the *social* level, human groups organise themselves at first by identifying a variety of functions that are needed for communal survival and well-being. Because the *group* has an interest in establishing and maintaining the order, individuals are taught their roles, and these lessons are reinforced with sanctions and honours. Likewise, *individuals* have a stake, not only because bare survival depends upon it, but also because psychologically we *identify* ourselves in terms of the roles that we occupy – as mother or father of these children, as graduate of that school, employee of a certain firm, leader in a given parish, etc.

Institutional definition of patterns of relationship has *a positive aspect*, insofar as it identifies them as socially useful, makes them public options, and provides social support (in the form of sanctions and honours). For example, during the twentieth century, marriage and the 'religious' life have been 'institutionalised' – recognised and reinforced by secular and canon law as well as by public opinion and reactions. Children have been encouraged imaginatively to 'try on' the roles of husband, wife, priest or nun; social structures are operative to train them for these roles. By contrast, except in closeted sub-cultures, same-sex sexual partnerships have not been institutionalised or benefited from legal or public support. Homosexual children have been left to their own devices, forced privately to discover the 'misfit' between socially certified options and their own inward dispositions, to wonder what might be wrong with them, to wrestle alone for integrity in their lives. The status of prostitution, the 'oldest profession', has been ambiguous: sometimes and in some places illegal, yet 'blind-eyed', recognised and entrenched; officially disapproved, but regularly patronised and accepted as a 'practical necessity'.

Society has understandably viewed sexual relationships as among the most important to organise and control, both because sexuality is among the strongest creative forces in human personality, and because it is linked – through the possibility for procreation – to the survival of the family, clan, ethnic group or nation. There has thus been a tendency to subsume it under the categories of purity and defilement, on the one hand, and taboo on the other.

Purity and defilement

Even in twentieth-century Europe and North America, sexual relationships were (to some extent still are) evaluated by the categories of purity and defilement. Thus, the traditional bride was supposed to be a *pure* virgin as was symbolised by her white dress. She was contrasted with a *'filthy whore'*. Likewise, rape was said to *defile* a woman. Various sorts of non-vaginal sexual activity were deemed *vile* and disgusting. Human sexuality itself was an *'off-colour'* subject – sexually allusive jokes and sexually explicit films were *dirty*.

Mary Douglas, in her book *Purity and Danger*, understands purity and defilement as social metaphors, part of a system of evaluation erected to enforce existing definitions and boundaries. 'Holy' means 'separate, having clear and distinct boundaries'; 'clean' signifies 'being wholly and completely a paradigm instance of a kind'; while 'dirt' refers to stuff out of order. There are many relevant orders – natural, social and liturgical. What lies outside or falls between the cracks of any order is *dangerous* because disruptive to the establishment, reminding us that human social grids always over-simplify and exclude things which – should they get too powerful – would overturn the present regime. What misfits is also *attractive* because it represents surplus power from the margins. Hence, witches, mediums, astrologers and desert hermits are viewed with a mixture of fear and fascination.

Natural orders function as metaphors of the social whole. When societies feel threatened, they develop elaborate rules about purity and pollution that make reference to natural taxonomies. Thus, in the Hebrew Bible, animals are regarded as unclean when they fail to fit into certain crude zoological categories; partly mildewed walls, splotchy skin and mixed-fibre cloth are unclean because they 'straddle', are neither wholly one thing nor the other. Likewise, because the human body is taken as a metaphor for the social whole, purity and defilement regulations collect around what goes into or comes out of the body. Thus, in the Hebrew Bible, much is made of the distinction between clean versus unclean foods (symbolic for who is admitted to and who excluded from membership in the society) and bodily discharge (menstrous women, ejaculating men and people with running sores are unclean insofar as they symbolise a breach or erosion of the social boundaries threatening the social unit with loss of definition). Unsurprisingly, bodily expressions of sexuality, which penetrate and violate the body's boundaries, become highly symbolic as well.

Taboos and their function

Threats to social order come in degrees – both concretely and symbolically. Refusal to respect property or physical safety is a *concrete* menace. Insofar as the sexual purity of women is a metaphor for social integrity, their failure to wear the veil may be seen as *a violation of the sacred* even though it may pose little concrete threat. Conditions that are not seriously disruptive, whether concretely or symbolically, may be set right via prescribed rituals – e.g., in Leviticus, menstrous women and ejaculating men may wash and contaminated silverware may be buried for a period of time.

Taboos are social structures erected to wall out behaviours and conditions that attack the social foundations. Because they aim to make the excluded behaviours or conditions *unthinkable*, they tend not to be rationalised or explained. To ask *why* already flirts with transgression. Likewise, there is no remedy for taboo violation. These behaviours and conditions make one unfit for polite society. They are so traitorous to social aims that the group is permanently unwilling to rehabilitate anyone who crosses the line. Thus, in ancient Israel, certain forms of adultery or incest were punishable by death. In 1980s California, the man who not only raped a woman but axed off her arms, could not find any community that was willing to receive him when he was released from prison.

Pollution and taboo are readily translated into divine sanction. After all, what most societies (not so) covertly regard as sacred is their own survival (this is still the premise of civil religion). The job description for the tribal deity is to secure and preserve the society of his/her devotees. Put otherwise, gods are supra-natural enforcers of social norms, the authors and defenders of taboos. The human authors of Leviticus and Numbers usher the Bible's God into this role as author of the holiness code and destroyer of abominations.

Some dynamics of social transition

Social consensus around sex and gender institutions starts to come undone when people start violating the taboos. Because taboos are inarticulate in their attempt to rule out behaviours and lifestyles as unthinkable, they have no answers to give when people start to re-examine what was so bad about such conduct, and are inadequate explanations of why conventional rules and role-expectations were granted a monopoly on wholesome ways to live. Insofar as individuals and groups see good in the formerly banned behaviours, they move forward to practise them. The more people raise questions, get poor answers, and enter into the experiment, the less social sanction is applied to the previously excluded practices and the more accepted they become.

The distinction between symbolic and concrete significance helps to explain the virulent illogic of reactions to taboo violations. Considered concretely, it is baffling how anyone could suppose that the homosexual practices of ten per cent (indeed the desire of a subset of gays and lesbians to be married and rear children) could explain the rise of the heterosexual divorce rate to fifty per cent and the consequent undermining of the nuclear family. Concretely, changes in heterosexual attitudes and behaviours will have to bear the lion's share of responsibility for that. The alleged relevance of homosexual activity to problems with heterosexual marriage and families is forged at the *symbolic* level. For to exclude practices by taboo is to assign them a high negative symbolic value: it is to say that the unspeakable behaviours and lifestyles are so dangerous as to threaten to undo the whole society. Add to this our individual psychological investment in conventional role definitions, which makes their unravelling threaten an end to who we are and to the positive meaning of our lives. It is a short and easy step to experience taboo violations as life-threatening, and to blame any and all social ills on whatever taboo violations are ready to hand!

Taboos and discernment

Taboos are enemies of Christian discernment for many reasons. First, because taboos make an idol of the *status quo*. Their function is to prop up merely human social systems, which invariably fall far short of the Kingdom of God. Merely human bodies politic are premised on scarcity; the Kingdom of God is based on divine bounty. Merely human societies buy luxury for some at the expense of others; the Kingdom of God will achieve utopic integration of individual flourishing with the common good. To the extent that taboos make change unthinkable, they obstruct human progress towards Kingdom-justice.

Second, taboos are enemies of Christian discernment insofar as they try to maintain social order through inarticulate fear, whereas the Kingdom of God is held together by the power and creativity of the Holy Spirit. Taboos spurn the divine Logos in their refusal to explain what is bad about what is forbidden or to suggest criteria for what would make sexual relationships good and wholesome and delightful. Likewise, taboos repress the image of God in human beings as persons capable of thought and choice, by forbidding us from bringing our sexuality up to consciousness for rational and prayerful examination.

Third, taboos are enemies of Christian discernment because they are in many ways immoral. Moral evaluations look to what a person intends and to what is within an agent's power. But from the point of view of taboo-maintenance or the holiness code, what is important is the 'objective' condition that a boundary was blurred or violated. Thus, the person who unwittingly steps on a grave or bumps into a menstrous woman is defiled willy nilly. Victims of incest or sexual assault are stained as much or even more so than the perpetrators (e.g., because female purity is symbolic of social integrity). Oedipus was ruined because he in fact married his mother, despite all of his conscious intentions and elaborate efforts to avoid it. Again, if taboos are enforced to secure the common good of social stability, they are unjust in making social misfits and straddlers pay a disproportionate share for the benefit of others. Indeed, the punishment exacted – of being cast into outer darkness with the attendant loss of personal dignity and wholeness, of community and concrete well-being, not because of any concrete harms one has actually inflicted on others, but rather because of what one *symbolises* – is cruel and unusual. It is made morally the worse by the fact that taboos exact this price without shouldering the responsibility to explain what is so 'out of the question' about the prohibited patterns. It becomes the more unchristian because misfitting social conventions could have re-creative rather than destructive potential!

Taboos are enemies of Christian discernment, but Christian Scriptures and traditions are human as well as divine and so bear the stamp of their many social contexts. In consulting them for normative guidance, the Church has to winnow, to thresh out the chaff of taboo from the wholesome grains of godward and godly advice!

Reclaiming incarnation

One common obstacle to clear Christian thinking about human sexuality is the deep alienation we feel between us and our bodies. Many of us have come, at least unconsciously, to believe that our bodies are not friends but enemies, burdens or at best tools. This conclusion may be thrust upon us naturally in the form of physical impairments: blindness, deafness, cerebral palsy, chemical imbalance compromising emotional control, arthritis, deteriorating joints, the torture of cancer or AIDS. Alternatively, our social experience of physical or sexual abuse may precipitate the divorce between person and body. We express this alienation in many ways: in hostility which punishes the body for its betrayal; or in denial that abstracts from its existence, hiding it in baggy clothes or shrinking it through anorexia; or in fear that wards off toxic attention with

layers of fat; or in despair that flaunts physical attractive-
ness, conceding that turf to the use and abuse of others, to
distract harmful notice from the 'real' person within.

The Church itself has fostered person–body polarisation
with its persistent misconstrual of St Paul's flesh–spirit
dichotomy, and its concomitant prohibition against dis-
cussing sex in the Church. As recently as a century ago,
English translations of the Ante-Nicene Fathers left their
discussions of sexual issues in Latin, so that they would be
accessible only to scholars. The result of such discretion has
not been high moral standards but rampant hypocrisy that
whispers soap-opera gossip while silencing education, that
produces alarming rates of sexual abuse and violence
within church nursery schools and the supposedly
Christian home. In North America, law suits have suc-
ceeded in getting the Church's attention. But its response
has been wooden. Instead of digging down to the roots of
our callings as sexual persons, it has set up superficial
training programmes as a hedge against prosecution and
advised clergy who are not licensed therapists to cut out
one-on-one time with youth and adults, thereby undermining pastoral care.

The Church's continual confusion of discipline with
repression is a great sin, bordering on apostasy. For the
alienation of body from person is contradicted by the central tenets of our Christian creed. God created a material
universe, made Adam living dust. Our Lord Jesus Christ
was no phantom but had a real human body, which really
suffered and really died. The Bible represents God's relation to his people, of Christ to the Church, with the sexual
image of marriage. Some views of eucharistic presence
even invite the conclusion that we can have carnal knowledge of God.

Clear Christian discernment about human sexuality
requires corrective lenses to overcome these distortions.
One such is the Church's own notion of a *sacrament*.
Human bodies – our own and others' – are *sacraments*, outward and visible signs, not merely material things pointing
to something else quite distinct from them (in the
Zwinglian manner), but participating symbols of *personal*
reality. Human bodies are *dimensions* of persons. One

corollary guideline for Christian discernment in times of
institutional change is that we should not treat human bodies as mere tools or dispensers of gratification. We should
reject the pretence that intimate bodily contact has no
impact on the person whose body it is. Indeed, for all but
the most cynical, the appeal of casual sex lies in its sacramental power to symbolise the embodied *personal* contact
that we all so deeply need.

Another corrective is St Paul's image of human bodies as
temples of the Holy Spirit. What is a temple but a place set
aside for honouring the holy? Of course, we Christians
believe that we should honour the holy everywhere, in all
that we are and have and do. Sacred space is merely the
stage on which we enact the rituals that give clearest
expression to our estimate of how valuable God is. St
Paul's phrase – *'temples* of the Holy Spirit' – reminds us that
we human beings are not just fancy organic computers
with capacities to calculate and speak. Rather, because the
Holy Spirit is so much the environment in which we live
and move and have our being, it evokes from us a capacity
to be spirit, fits us not only to interact with other human
beings but also to be lovers of God. The Holy Spirit of God
has so built itself into the functional centre of who we are,
that we quite literally are sacred, because the sacred has
quite literally made its dwelling place with us.

This conception yields a second guideline for Christian
discernment in the midst of institutional flux: that is, that
we should not do to another human body, or allow to be
done to our own bodies, anything that would not be honouring to Christ. The Bible teaches that human sexual
encounters are potential *acts of worship* with its reports of
divine commands to be fruitful and multiply and to make
love on the Sabbath day. Conversely, human sexual acts
desecrate the temple when they are abusive or are parts of
relationships (even marriages) that deface the image of
Christ in either person. Likewise, we *blaspheme* when we
allow our bodies to be tokens of exchange in relationships
premised on despair that wholesome personal intimacy is
possible.

Discerning discipline, disciplined discernment

Christian teaching on human sexuality has always sounded the theme of *discipline*. But in times of social transition, discipline is not a matter of holding fast to traditional rules or forcing oneself and others into the moulds of past institutions. Rather it is a matter of teachability, of sensitivity, alertness and openness to learn, of courage to profit from experience.

In the winds of change, taboos are enemies of discipline, because they stop up our ears and shut tight our eyes. Insisting on taboos shirks Christian responsibility to take a critical look at heterosexual marriage and celibacy, to see how these institutions have not only fostered human flourishing but also cramped our styles, and to consider how they might be revitalised and improved. For more than several decades, many serious Christians have been colouring outside the lines of past norms. It is time to digest the results of the lifestyle experiments they have tried: e.g., to consider what was helpful and what hurtful; to reflect on the many dimensions of human intimacy, on what happens when they are woven together, on what emerges when they are teased apart. Yet, vigorous reassertion that heterosexual marriage and celibacy are the only paths to righteousness, will disincline experimenters to share what they have learned with the Church. Worse yet, it will give them the impression that they can't afford to bring their sexuality into their relationship with God, and pressure them into spiritual fragmentation. To tell the truth, taboo-approaches to sexuality tend to keep everyone in the closet as sexual persons, to send the message that we can't afford to be honest with anyone, lest we expose something that will cast us into outer darkness as well!

To explore new territory requires courage to believe that we are justified by faith and not by correctness of belief or practice. It moves from the conviction that our creator knows our limitations, does not expect us everywhere and always to get things right, but is eager to work with us as partners in the honest and searching discernment to which God calls us. It requires trust in God to suspend judgement in the interests of coming to a more complicated and nuanced picture and of evolving a wider range of subtler institutions.

Happily, our liturgy offers another image, in the neighbourhood of sacrament and temple, that helps us distinguish holy experiments from *laissez-faire* self-indulgence and despair. In holy experiments, we offer 'ourselves, our souls and bodies' to God 'as a living sacrifice'. In sacrificial rites, the offering is laid out on the altar in plain sight of God and the human beings involved. Prayers are said, asking God to accept the offering and to bless those who bring it – to forgive where they have gone wrong, to redirect fresh efforts, and to prosper promising beginnings. So, too, we Christians are called to offer ourselves, our souls and bodies, most especially our sexual relationships, by bringing them out in the open with God and begging to know what God thinks of them. In the absence of established institutions, how else are gay and lesbian Christians to arrive at wholesome patterns of life together except by trying experiments and praying them through? In these changing times, the conventionally married and celibate need to join in the same liturgy, if the Church's traditional institutions are to be renewed. Watched, prayed, and offered sexuality stands a chance of winning through to a deeper appreciation of what God meant in creating us as sexual persons in the first place. Because such priestly self-sacrifice of sexuality brings everything out of the closet into the light of Christ, it may gain insight into why current institutions are unravelling, and gather clues towards a richer reintegration in the future. And so there is a third corollary for Christian discernment in winds of change: *let the posture of priestly offering displace and abolish the enforcement of taboos!*

© 2005 Marilyn McCord Adams

4 Marriage, sexuality and the Christian tradition

Jane Shaw

Introduction: the Christian tradition

In the current debates about sexuality in the Church, the common perception is that there are two schools of thought. The first, so the story goes, holds fast to Scripture and the Christian tradition in its advocacy of marriage as the norm for Christian life, and indeed often identifies itself as 'traditionalist', while the second wishes to introduce liberal ideas (toleration of homosexuality, most obviously), largely on the basis of secular ideas of justice and human rights. These two groups are seen as being at loggerheads with one another, apparently with little common ground, despite their shared Christian faith.

This common perception is mistaken. First, it suggests that only one of these positions takes a 'traditional Christian' stand. This is inaccurate – though it is a highly effective ideological claim for those who wish to claim their position as the Truth. It is more accurate to say that each reads Scripture faithfully and seriously, and attends to the tradition, but comes to different conclusions. Secondly, it suggests that there are only two positions – of course, there are many variations in between these two poles. Thirdly, it works with an understanding of the Christian tradition as static and unchanging. The Christian tradition is not static, though some wish to claim that it is. It is, rather, dynamic. This means that the Church's attitudes – even its official statements – on sexuality, marriage and related questions are not only in flux now, but have shifted and changed over two thousand years of history.

There are three major reasons why the tradition is not

and cannot be static. First, if we take the Christian doctrine of the incarnation seriously, then we can say that the Christian God is profoundly interested in what is happening in the world, to the extent that he participated in its mess and muddle as the man Jesus of Nazareth. This is the key to the divine–human relationship. Nor was it a one-off event in Jesus, but it is sustained in the third person of the Godhead, the Holy Spirit, who – we are promised in the Scriptures – is always at work in the world. Our task lies in discerning how and when that happens. Second, hermeneutics – how we interpret things – suggests that in reading Scripture (or any text for that matter) we each bring our questions to the text; indeed, we need to, in order to bring the text alive, to give it meaning, to understand it. I don't understand a physics textbook because I have no questions to bring to it, having given up physics aged sixteen with a sigh of relief. However, we can all grapple with and read Scripture because we have the questions of our life to bring to it – it is those questions that bring the biblical stories alive. Christian tradition is the repeated interpretation of Scripture and its outworking in the life and practice of the Church and the lives of individual Christians. Each generation or community therefore *necessarily* interprets Scripture afresh in the light of its own experiences, and puts its insights from Scripture into practice in a range of ways. Third, Christianity always and necessarily interacts with culture. Despite the Church's or particular Christians' attempts to remain entirely 'unworldly' – at least at certain times and places – Christianity has always helped shape, and has in turn been shaped by, the larger culture. This means that all the Church's thinking has changed over 2000 years. *Traditio* is about the process of handing down from one generation to another, but each generation necessarily reads Scripture and tradition through its own spectacles and lives it in its own culture. Just as this has happened with the Church's ideas about slavery or salvation or the nature of the priesthood, so it has happened with its ideas about sexuality and marriage. The Church's thinking on these matters has not been univocal. The Church, historically, has been concerned not with heterosexual marriage vs. homosexuality –

that is a recent obsession – but with the question of marriage vs. celibacy. As the historian Diarmaid MacCulloch has put it, 'The greatest fault-line in Christian attitudes to sex lies in the status of virginity and celibacy relative to heterosexual marriage.'[1] This suggests, then, that marriage has not always had the status it apparently enjoys today, in most Christian circles, a status that is thought by many always to have been the 'norm'.

This essay looks first at the history of marriage vs. celibacy; then at changing Christian attitudes to marriage and celibacy; and then finally and briefly at both the role of friendship and the question of homosexuality, in relation to Christian ideas about marriage. It also aims to offer a complementary perspective to that of Robert Merrihew Adams who, in his essay in this volume, argues from a philosophical perspective, that to appeal to the 'natural' and the 'unnatural' is always dangerous territory. For historians, the categories of 'natural' and the 'unnatural' are also to be treated with caution, for a little historical digging shows that one person's 'natural' at one moment is another person's 'unnatural' at another.

Marriage vs. celibacy

It is commonplace in many Church documents today – ranging from *Some Issues in Human Sexuality* (the Church of England's 2003 report)[2] to various statements on human sexuality made by meetings of the Lambeth Conference (most notably those of 1978 and 1998) to the Windsor report of 2004 – to state, or work upon the assumption, that lifelong (heterosexual) marriage is and always has been the 'norm'. Marriage is therefore invoked as something unchanging – always the norm in the Christian tradition, and always recognisably the same. This begs some questions: Has marriage always been the prevailing norm in the Christian tradition? What do such documents mean by marriage? Does our modern understanding of marriage bear any resemblance to the reality of marriage for our Christian forbears?

If we return to our beginnings, and to the life and teaching of the emerging Church in the first two or three centuries of Christianity, we find that with far-flung churches and widely differing worshipping communities, diversity of practice and teaching was a hallmark of the Early Church. This was as true of Christians' ideas about sexuality and marriage as it was of their ideas about the Eucharist or baptism. The early churches engaged with a number of texts about marriage, monogamy and celibacy, most notably Matthew 19, Mark 10 and 1 Corinthians 7. In some parts of the world, Christians also engaged with Gnostic ideas, practices and writings, such as the Gospel of Thomas, which were fiercely ascetical, and profoundly dualistic in their understanding of spirit and body. Some historians have suggested that early Christians lived either with a sense of Christ's imminent second coming or with the sense that they were building the Kingdom of God here and now, and this apocalyptic view led some to ask whether relationships such as those formed in the bonds of marriage were to exist in the new age. A wide range of views therefore existed as they reached for a sense of what a Christian ethic might be, and grappled with what might be workable in terms of Church policy in the face of divergent practices.

In Mark 10 and Matthew 19, Jesus talks about divorce. In Mark, there is an absolute prohibition of divorce; in Matthew a concession is provided. In Mark, there is a sense of the parallel obligations of man and woman; neither can initiate divorce. In Matthew, the man may initiate divorce for unchastity or 'uncleanness'. Mark's gospel was written before Matthew's, and we do not know why Matthew changed the text here to portray Jesus as giving this particular concession. New Testament scholars have struggled with this at some length. Maybe Matthew was self-consciously reflecting church policy? Certainly, as Peter Coleman writes, 'the variation in the texts suggests that the early church was uncertain what to do about the consequences of broken marriages.'[3]

Uppermost in the minds of those who wrote favourably about marriage were, therefore, the related themes of monogamy and the nature of lifelong marriage. Probably the most positive view of marriage in this period is that provided by Clement of Alexandria (150–215 CE) who saw it as an equal calling with celibacy. In Chapter XII of 'On Marriage' (in his *Miscellanies* Book III), he wrote that both celibacy and marriage have their own different forms of service and ministry to the Lord. While he (like other writers) certainly saw marriage as a place in which sexual desire could be focused and therefore rightly ordered, Clement also saw positive characteristics, which could be developed in marriage. Writing to the male householder (his primary audience), he made it clear that these positive characteristics included caring for one's wife and children and taking responsibility for everything in the home shared with a wife. (Not surprisingly, here Clement appeals to 1 Timothy 3:4ff, in which the ideal bishop is said to be a responsible householder.) A married man is therefore able to give a distinctive Christian service, which the single man cannot, in the household.

Tertullian (160–225 CE) – Clement's contemporary – wrote on monogamy, in a letter to his wife (*Ad Uxorem*, c.205) in which he asked that she not marry after his death. Tertullian emphasised the bond of monogamous marriage, the sentimental attachment between man and woman; indeed he went so far as to say that the best things about marriage were loyalty, friendship and companionship – especially when (he claimed!) you had grown old enough to cease (or cease wanting) sexual activity. Remarriage was therefore unthinkable because of this strong bond which was irreplaceable and unique, unbroken by death. He looked, as did so many others at the time, to the resurrection of the body and therefore to being united with his wife in the life of the saints gathered, a state in which they would be restored into angelic holiness. In his *Exhortation to Chastity*, his imagined reader was an older widower who would not be tempted to give in to sexual urges, but did have to be warned against remarriage: in the young, it was the sexual urge that had to be controlled, whereas in the old it was this possible wandering into another marriage for the purposes of companionship which needed to be stopped. Later in life, Tertullian joined a group that combined rather strict ascetical practices with an attempt to live by the guidance of the Spirit, namely, Montanism.

The Montanists were just one of several groups in

second- and third-century Christian culture that advocated celibacy and an ascetic lifestyle. In the hills of Asia Minor and Syria for example, there were groups of encratites, men and women who lived 'in continence' with one another, abstaining from all sexual intercourse (even if married), and taking on other ascetical practices, including dietary restraints (no meat, no wine). For them, marriage and sexual union were signs of the 'present age', of mortality, of continuing poverty, pride and decay; they looked, rather, to the new age. Cessation from sexual activity was one of the things that signalled redemption from the present age. These sorts of views are found in Gnostic texts, such as the *Gospel of Thomas*, a second-century text that circulated (especially in Syria and Egypt) for several centuries and then disappeared until rediscovered in 1945. The goal of this kind of Christian morality was to disconnect oneself from the world (which was seen as a 'corpse') and 'the world' included all social structures, including family relations. As Wayne Meeks puts it, 'the body is the switching point where one meets the world and where one must break the connection.'[4]

What was the right way forward? This was the question for the early churches. Was marriage to be the Christian norm – as it was in the wider, pagan society? Or, for Christians, should celibacy be the norm, the higher ideal for which to strive? The clash between the views and practices of Clement of Alexandria and the encratites illustrates the tension. The seemingly extreme views of the encratites marked a growing move towards viewing celibacy as the higher good, and we can sense, in Clement's writings, the threat to marriage (as an equal calling with celibacy) which that posed. In the *Instructor (Paedagogus)*, a detailed manual addressed to new Christians telling them how to behave in all matters from dress to sexual relations, we see Clement reassuring the married householder that his way of life is acceptable. He discussed the encratites at length, refuting their arguments; if they had been merely marginal he need not have done this. Most likely, however, he and the members of his church encountered them frequently as they walked down from the hills into Alexandria. One can imagine the encratites wagging their fingers with judgement at the 'moderate' married Christians in the streets. As Peter Brown puts it, 'Encratite arguments against sex demanded answers from the very heart of the marriage bed.'[5]

The interpretation of one particular biblical text was key in this struggle to discern the way forward: 1 Corinthians 7, especially verses 7 to 9. Here Paul writes, 'I wish that all were as I myself am. But each has a particular gift from God, one having one kind and another a different kind. To the unmarried and widows I say that it is well for them to remain unmarried as I am. But if they are not practising self-control, they should marry. For it is better to marry than to be aflame with passion' (NRSV). Did Paul mean that the higher good, the ideal to which all should aspire, is celibacy? Is marriage therefore a second best, something to which one resorts if one cannot control one's lust? Or did he really mean that different people have different gifts – of celibacy and marriage – and that these are equally valid? These questions of interpretation have been argued about throughout Christian history, but by the fourth century the majority of learned and leading Christians were quite clear what the answer was: celibacy was the higher good, marriage was second best. This would remain the Church's attitude for over a thousand years. A particular interpretation of the first part of verse 7 of 1 Corinthians 7 had won out: 'I wish that all were as I myself am.'

Every age has its questions and, for the early Christians, these were their questions about human sexuality. Their first question was about the meaning of monogamy. The lifelong and monogamous nature of marriage advocated by Jesus ruled out divorce; did it also mean, as Tertullian suggested, that widows and widowers should not remarry? Their second question, formulated in response to 1 Corinthians 7:7-9, was this: Was marriage or celibacy the higher good, the Christian ideal, for which to strive?

Celibacy

By the fourth century, marriage was no longer considered 'the norm' for Christians, if it ever had been. The Church had taken a distinctive stance against the values of the world, the wider society, and was teaching that the ideal was celibacy (the single life) combined with sexual asceticism (as part of a broader ascetical practice). Only two people wrote on the good of marriage in this period, one was a rather mad monk named Jovinian, and the other was Augustine – whose own response to a conjugal partnership was not entirely positive (he left the woman with whom he had lived, for about thirteen years from the age of seventeen or eighteen, and had a son, and his *Confessions* document his attempts to control his strong sexual drive). Nevertheless, through his exposition of the three goods of marriage (offspring, fidelity and the sacramental bond), Augustine exercised an influence on Christian thinking about marriage long after his own time: for example, these three goods formed the basis of *Casti Connubii*, the 1930 Roman Catholic document on marriage, opposing the use of contraception. Nevertheless, all the other main patristic writers of late antiquity, in the East and West, from Ambrose to Gregory of Nyssa, wrote in favour of holy virginity and in defence of celibacy as the greater good. It is perhaps not too hard to understand why. With the toleration of Christianity under Constantine, and Christianity's official status by the end of the fourth century, Christians had no way of marking themselves out as different from the status quo, whereas persecution and martyrdom in the early centuries of the Church had certainly indicated that Christians were a distinctive people, willing to die for their faith. Some historians have suggested that celibacy was a substitute for martyrdom as a way of becoming the most perfect sort of Christian. Furthermore, the kinds of people who looked suitable to be a bishop in the fourth and fifth centuries were no longer slaves or artisans, but men like Ambrose, Governor of Milan, from a powerful Italian family. How might they distinguish themselves from other state officials? Celibacy and an ascetic lifestyle were one answer. The notion that marriage was lifelong became fudged, not for the modern reasons that we wish to tolerate divorce or allow widows and widowers to remarry, but for the prevailing Christian ideal of the greater good: wives were put to one side so that both bishop and wife might be celibate, and live as brother and sister.

This was the age in which the ascetic tradition developed. Desert asceticism was exemplified by the life of St Anthony and soon grew in popularity, to such an extent that some complained that the desert was getting too crowded. It was also the moment when the monastic tradition emerged, beginning with men such as Pachomius who set up monasteries along the banks of the Nile in the early fourth century, and Benedict, the 'father' of western monasticism, whose Rule, written in the sixth century, became immensely influential.

Both women and men lived the celibate life in a variety of formal and less formal settings, sometimes as solitaries in the desert, sometimes in monastic communities, and sometimes, for women, as dedicated holy virgins living in households in the city. Some of the Church Fathers' sayings – notably Jerome's – are notoriously misogynistic, but it may be that a life of holy virginity was liberating for women. It was, of course, mostly elite women who took on this way of life, and by doing so they opted out of a set of social structures in which they were passed from father to husband in an arranged marriage which was about the exchange or uniting of property and the production of male heirs. By living with other dedicated virgins and widows, they often came to wield considerable spiritual and even economic power – the example of Gregory of Nyssa's sister, Macrina, comes to mind – and exercise an otherwise unknown independence. This was not always popular with their families, who saw lost opportunities for dynastic alliances: Ambrose's treatise on virginity of the late fourth century was written with this in mind, and he urged young women to resist their families' schemes for marriage and take the higher path. The celibate way of life was not only regarded as the higher way, but also as properly counter-cultural at a moment when the Church was becoming more fused with the state in so many other areas.

Between the fourth and fourteenth centuries, society changed radically in its structures and attitudes. Nevertheless, this ideal of celibacy as the higher good endured, as illustrated by the life of Margery Kempe who, unusually for the time, dictated her story to a scribe: this was *The Book of Margery Kempe* and remains a rare account from this period of a woman's spiritual life, emotions and values. She was the daughter of the mayor of Lynn (later King's Lynn) in Norfolk and in 1393 married a Lynn burgess, John Kempe. She pleaded with him that they might lead 'continent' lives, for she wished to be a dedicated holy virgin within her marriage. Virginity was defined not only as a physical state but also as a moral and spiritual state, 'that quality of spirit belonging to those whose primary relationship is with God'.[6] Her husband eventually relented, but only after twenty years of marriage and the birth of fourteen children. She was then able to go on pilgrimage to Compostela and other pilgrimage sites, and was given the gift of holy tears as well as mystical experiences.

The example of Kempe shows the persistence of this paradigm – that celibacy was the higher good – over a long period. One of the key themes of this long period when celibacy was regarded as the greater good was the development of the distinctive idea that the clergy and the dedicated religious were set apart from the laity. It was, of course, recognised that the vast majority of the population would not take this higher path. Celibate clergy, as well as monks and nuns who were not ordained, were therefore meant to be the standard-bearers of morals, not only in their teaching but also in their personal way of life. Some lay people, such as Kempe, wished to emulate them. While the vast majority of the population might be 'doomed' to marriage, and the medieval Church gradually began to take some control of how marriage occurred (reiterating that it was a sacrament), the clergy, monks and nuns were perceived as exemplifying the most perfect form of Christian discipleship by their celibacy. This view was reiterated in numerous Church councils, and the great reformer of the church, Gregory VII, in the eleventh century finally made official and explicit that which had been at least implicit for several centuries – that clergy should remain unmarried and celibate. It is important to acknowledge, however, that celibacy was not always practised by priests; bishops (who themselves did not always follow the Church's teaching on this) often preferred to ignore the problem, or make money by taxing rather than disciplining those non-celibate clergy who came to their attention. As we shall see in a moment, Martin Luther in the sixteenth century pointed to this disparity between teaching and practice, calling the Church to follow practice rather than ideal by allowing clergy to marry, arguing that not all were called to celibacy and that it was better for men and women (he was thinking of nuns) to be married (and mono- gamous) than engage in sexual relationships outside marriage.

It is worth noting at this point, that this presumption that the clergy should be held to a different standard of moral behaviour from that required of lay people, while having been shattered at the Reformation, and largely (and delib- erately) dispelled in the modern Church, which has emphasised lay and ordained people's common baptism, has stayed around in Britain in current teaching about homosexuality and the priesthood, as for example, in the 1991 Church of England House of Bishops document, *Issues in Human Sexuality*, which holds gay and lesbian clergy to a different standard of sexual behaviour than gay and lesbian lay people. (This is reiterated in the 2003 docu- ment, *Some Issues in Human Sexuality*.) This notion of com- pulsory celibacy without the *vocation* to celibacy, advocated for gay and lesbian clergy in our own day, is inherited from the periods of antiquity and the Middle Ages. Some people are therefore calling the Church to honesty, as Luther did, by allowing its gay and lesbian clergy to live in monoga- mous and permanent same-sex relationships, In our own day, we are then, in some ways, replaying an argument that was fought out in the Protestant Reformation about mar- riage, celibacy and vocation; we therefore now turn to that period in order to understand the nature of those changes.

Marriage and family

It was Martin Luther who shattered the idea that the clergy should be set apart from the laity, with his notion of the priesthood of all believers. If all stand equally before God, why could priests not marry? Why should those who are called to priesthood but not to celibacy be forced to remain celibate? This is what he began to preach in the 1520s. He,

Zwingli in Zurich, and other Protestant reformers over-
turned the longstanding paradigm that saw celibacy as
better than marriage, and not only preached but also practised what they taught by defiantly marrying. In this, they
initiated an extraordinary paradigm shift in the Church's
thinking and teaching.

This 180-degree turn was based on a new reading of
Scripture, in particular of 1 Corinthians 7:7-9. If the patristic writers emphasised the first part of verse 7, Luther now
focused on verse 8: 'it is better to marry than to be aflame
with passion', supporting it in numerous sermons with
verse 2, 'because of sexual immorality, each man should
have his own wife, and each woman her own husband.'
This was a 'negative' argument in favour of marriage: the
regulation of sexual desire, a theme that had also been a
preoccupation of those in the Early Church who had written in support of marriage, such as Augustine. In some
cases, this was the only or the main justification of clergy
marriage, as for example in the legislation that permitted it
in the English Church in the Protestant King Edward VI's
reign, in 1549. The statute noted that it was better for ministers in the Church of God to live 'chaste, sole and separate
from the company of women and the bond of marriage'
because then they would be less troubled with the charge
of a household and could attend to the administration of
the Gospel better. However, 'such uncleanness of living,
and other great inconveniences . . . have followed of com-
pelled chastity' that it was thought better, after consultation with the Scripture, that the commonwealth suffer
ministers 'to live in holy marriage, than feignedly abuse
with worse enormity outward chastity or single life'.[7]

Luther and other reformers, including later Protestant
writers in England, also offered a more positive theology of
the estate of marriage, turning to the creation accounts in
Genesis and arguing that man and woman were not meant
to be alone but were to enjoy the companionship that marriage allowed, as well as the virtues of marital sex.
Ironically, of course, marriage had been a sacrament for
the medieval Church, which valued it less, while under the
reformers it was no longer a sacrament despite the new
emphasis on its importance. Furthermore, it took a while

for the idea of married priests to take hold: in England, Elizabeth I was famously opposed to clergy marrying, especially her bishops (whose marriages she did not recognise), and people sometimes refused to receive communion from married clergymen. For so long, marriage had been seen as distinctly second-class from a Christian point of view, that people now had difficulty discerning the difference between the wife now living in the pastor's house and the 'mistress' the old priest used to keep. The Protestant reformers had a long way to go in making marriage (for themselves) not only the higher good (above celibacy) but even respectable!

In short, marriage still needed a good press; the Protestant reformers were very busy, not only in preaching and writing pamphlets, but in placing the godly household at the centre of their practical reforms. They therefore began to represent marriage as a cornerstone of society, an institution upon which all other institutions might be built. This new emphasis on the married household even came to be seen as one of the appeals of Protestantism: the historian Lyndal Roper has suggested that the urban 'middling sorts' who took on the Protestant reforming ideas, and implemented them in the cities of Germany, were those who most stood to benefit from the arrangement of such a household.[8] However, we must remember that we are not here talking about the modern marriage unit of husband and wife and children so often invoked in reports on human sexuality in our own day, but rather about the *household*: this consisted of husband and wife, children, servants, and often apprentices. There was little separation between home and work: the two were intertwined in household workshops. This household was hierarchically arranged with the father/husband/master in charge, and wife, children and servants/apprentices in descending order beneath his control. (This household arrangement goes back to antiquity, and was advocated, for example, in Aristotle's *Politics*.) The new Protestant emphasis on marriage therefore suited the male head of such a household, for it justified the particular arrangement of his living and working conditions and reinforced his authority within them – though the large number of prescriptive manuals

61

telling people how to arrange and behave in such house-holds, as well as city ordinances legislating these ideals, suggests that members of the household needed a lot of prompting as to how they ought to behave! Keeping order was important because the household was envisioned as a 'little commonwealth', a microcosm of the larger society, the nation and ultimately even the order of the universe. If something went out of kilter in the household then it could and would affect the larger world (think of King Lear giv-ing away his property before he died and how wrong everything subsequently went). The 'private' family of the modern world did not yet exist. There was, however, often a tension between prescription and practice: when the Puritan preacher William Gouge delivered his lectures *Of Domesticall Duties* at Blackfriars in early seventeenth-century London, women in the congregation heckled him when he advocated the beating of wives to keep them in line.

This example illustrates a tension in this paradigm. There was much talk about the mutuality of the husband and wife; they were portrayed as 'helpmeets'; there was now a new emphasis on the choosing of one's spouse; and in some seventeenth-century Puritan writings we find an attempt to invest marriage with a notion of ongoing romantic attachment. Gouge even went so far as to say that the wife was a joint governor in the household with her husband. At the same time, a great deal of emphasis was placed on male authority or headship, and on Paul's mes-sage about the submission of women. This paradox was inevitable, given the prevailing biological understandings of man and woman at this time. Relying still on the ancient sources of Aristotle and Galen, scientists understood woman as an imperfect version of man; that is, there was 'one sex' hierarchically arranged. It was thought that men and women had exactly the same genitals, but women's were imperfectly formed and therefore remained inside. This fitted well with Aristotle's notion, which was also prevalent, that female bodies are formed because of deficient heat in the reproductive process (i.e. they did not quite make it to being men). Medieval theologians such as Aquinas took up these arguments in their understanding of human nature, arguing nevertheless that it was still natural to the species that there should be both male and female. These ideas about women and men were widespread, even in popular culture, as evidenced by folk tales from this era of women who jumped over fences, with the result that their genitals dropped and they became men. The historian Thomas Laqueur has named this the 'one-sex model'.[9] What this illustrates is that women were seen to fit into the hierarchical nature of the household easily, given prevailing medical understandings of their 'nature' in relationship to men. Protestant reformers took over these ideas, for they were not to be challenged until the Enlightenment, some two hundred years later. It is to that modern era that we now turn.

The birth of the modern family

It is only when we get to the modern era, in the eighteenth century and after, that we can begin to see ideas and patterns of marriage and family, and even understandings of who women and men are, with which we identify today. The shifts that led to our modern understandings of marriage and ideas about men and women were largely socially and even economically driven, but they came to be readily taken up by the churches. When we think of marriage and family today, and when 'traditional marriage' is invoked in Church documents as the Christian norm, it is in fact to a relatively modern notion of marriage that our minds turn. Such marriage is seen as constituting part of a 'family', imagined as a limited number of people (husband and wife, children) who live in a unit quite separate from others to whom they might be related or with whom they might have friendship or work ties. Such an idea of 'family' was largely a product of the Industrial Revolution, in the late eighteenth and nineteenth centuries, for only then was work taken away from the home. Economic conditions created new understandings of a split between 'private' and 'public' and also produced 'class' as we think of it today. The 'working classes' – both men and women, and even children – now went out to work; the aristocracy and gentry did what they had always done; and the middle classes emerged as a new force, in some ways the main 'trendsetters' of the time. For in the middle classes the ideal, at least, was that the men went out to work, but women stayed at home. These shifts produced new domestic arrangements as a new role was given to women: they were now seen as inhabiting the private sphere, guarding not only hearth and home but also family morals, while men went out into the cut and thrust of public life. They were, in the famous phrase coined by the poet Coventry Patmore, the 'angels in the house'.

Science also weighed in. While formerly scientists had turned to the ancient sources, Aristotle and Galen, to see women as inferior versions of men in their biological make-up, now they began to see women as distinctly different creatures. Scientists sought difference in women's anatomy and physiology; sometimes they found it, sometimes they didn't, but they certainly taught it. Thus women's exclusion from the public sphere and the professional workforce came to be justified on the 'scientific' grounds that they were 'naturally' weaker than men. In short, a notion of 'sexual difference' was promulgated in a way that it never had been before or, as historian Thomas Laqueur puts it, this period gave birth to the 'two-sex model'. In particular, the notion of the complementarity of the sexes came to prevail – that is, that women and men have distinctly different qualities (and that these are rooted in biology) and this suits them for different (but 'complementary') roles in life. Men were seen as hardy and robust with an aggressive sexual appetite, while women were portrayed as frail, rather prone to weakness and sexually passive. This was a dramatic shift from understandings of female sexuality in the pre-modern era where it was generally believed that both women and men had to emit 'seed' (that is, have orgasms) for conception to take place.

Of course this was all prescriptive, seeking to mould the behaviour of women and men, propounded in a range of literature, from household manuals to etiquette books to sermons. It did not necessarily match what people did in real life, but a new and powerful ideology had been shaped and it held a strong grip, not least amongst the evangelical middle classes. The churches readily took on these ideas about marriage, family, men and women – even though such ideas largely emerged from the political, social, economic and scientific worlds – and gave them theological underpinning.[10] A popular Christian writer on this topic in the nineteenth century was John Angell James, one of the most well-known Congregationalist ministers of his day and a leading figure in the evangelical revival. His *Female Piety* (1853) articulated in theological terms many of these new ideas about women's proper sphere, and argued strongly against women 'sullying' themselves in the world of public work. He wrote, 'Christianity has provided a place for woman for which she is fitted [the home], and in which she shines; but take her out of that place, and her lustre pales and sheds a feeble and sickly ray.' He continued,

> The Bible gives her her place of majesty and dignity in the domestic circle: that is the heart of her husband and the heart of her family . . . A woman who fills well the sphere assigned to her, as a wife, a mother, and a mistress; who trains up good citizens for the state, and good fathers and mothers of other families which are to spring from her own; and so from generation to generation in all but endless succession, need not complain that her sphere of action and her power of influence are too limited for female ambition to aspire to.

As Angell James' work illustrates, Pauline notions of female submission were made to fit with gender complementarity just as they had with older notions of gender hierarchy. 'Woman scarcely needs to be taught, that in the domestic economy she is second, and not first, that "the man is the head of the woman." This is a law of nature written on the heart, and coincides exactly with the law of God written on the page of revelation. It is first of all an instinct, and then confirmed by reason.' Woman 'instinctively' knew all of this; it was in her nature: 'She generally knows her place, and feels it her happiness as well as her duty to keep it. It is not necessity but even choice that produces a willing subjection. She is contented it should be so, for God has implanted the disposition in her nature.'[11] The result was not so much that sexual complementarity meant 'different and equal', as so often claimed, but rather 'different and entirely unequal'.

While we recognise the language of 'spheres' and 'complementarity', because they are sometimes used in our own day, and while we can see the roots of modern ideas of marriage in the eighteenth and nineteenth centuries, we also recognise that ideas of marriage and family have continued to change since then. We should remember that the middle-class Victorian family did not just consist of husband, wife and children, but also servants; servants were an expected part of the middle-class household until well after World War I in Britain. The expectation that the family unit will consist of the married couple and a limited number of children is one of twentieth-century origin. Our own reality is that we can control the number of children that we have by use of reliable birth control and/or reproductive technology. Indeed, the Church seriously wrestled with the question of whether it should accept birth control when its use was becoming more widespread in the early twentieth century. At the 1908 Lambeth Conference, the Anglican bishops followed the general tone of 'respectable' intellectual and medical debate in England, finding it abhorrent:

> The conference regards with alarm the growing practice of the artificial restrictions of the family, and earnestly calls upon all Christian people to discountenance the use of all artificial means of restriction as demoralising to character and hostile to national welfare.[12]

The 1920 Lambeth Conference held to this line. But in 1930 an extraordinary sea change occurred: the Anglican bishops decided that birth control was acceptable, at least in a limited way for married couples. This is interesting for our purposes because it illustrates another occasion in which the Church followed society, in a fairly rapid shift of thinking. For Christian theologies of marriage up until that point had largely followed Augustine's three goods and these were necessarily intertwined: offspring, fidelity and companionship. Now, there was the possibility that one of these goods could be deliberately omitted from the marriage: offspring. Once this was permitted, the prohibition of sexual activity between two adults where sexual activity was clearly for the purpose of companionship, for the forging of a union of love, and yet where procreation was not possible – that is between two men or between two women – became much more difficult to sustain in Christian terms, as arguments in the late twentieth- and early twenty-first-century church illustrate, but that was, quite frankly, probably not a consequence foreseen by the Anglican bishops in 1930! Similarly, patterns of divorce have changed and, as the wider society has become more accepting of divorce, so have the churches.

We should not forget, either, that the changing role of women in the twentieth century has had an impact on changing patterns of marriage. This is often presented by more conservative Christian writers as something which we should regret: if only women had not messed everything up . . . There are two key things to be said in the response to this. First, as we have seen, the idea of women staying at home in a 'traditional' marriage really only stems from the late eighteenth and the nineteenth centuries when economic and social arrangements made this the desirable (middle-class) norm. Secondly, as we survey Christian writings on marriage and sexuality over two thousand years, we find that although there are two sexes, only one has written very much in this area. Men have spoken for both men and women in the Christian tradition, on sexuality as on so much else; it is, however, particularly ironic in the area of sexuality, for men can never experience sexuality as women do, and vice versa, and the misunderstandings men have had about women have often caused difficulties to say the least. For example, Augustine's ideas about marriage have been central to Christian teaching on the subject, binding for both men and women, but Augustine himself presents a series of very mixed messages about women. As Henry Chadwick sums it up,

> He opposed the current exposition of St Paul's words (1 Cor. 11:7) according to which the male, not the female, is made in God's image. He held that women and men are differentiated in body, not in soul or powers of mind. On the other hand, he took it to be self-evident that the prime function of a woman is

biological . . . He assumed that in marriage the wife's role is to be domestic and supportive.

Chadwick goes on to argue that Augustine's sayings illustrate the commonplace that generalised attitudes to women are often determined by attitudes to sexuality, and wryly comments of Augustine that 'The man who had once adhered to the ascetic Manichees and simultaneously lived with a woman to meet his erotic need could be expected to be inconsistent.' In short, we need to ask how we should evaluate the teachings on marriage of a man who 'feared sexuality (not least in himself) as passing easily out of rational control. Even the sisters in the Hippo nunnery were warned that a woman can unconsciously and unintentionally throw a man off balance merely by a flashing eye.'[13] The example of the Puritan writers of the early seventeenth century is also instructive: while they advocated mutuality in marriage and re-emphasised the affective bond between husband and wife, as we have seen they struggled with the presuppositions of their own day that woman was inferior to man and should, if necessary, be disciplined to keep order in the hierarchically arranged household. We could, of course, turn to many more examples. Suffice it to say, that twentieth-century feminist critiques of many of the presuppositions about the place of women and men in Christian marriage have much to teach the Church, and the churches should not be afraid of listening to women and taking on board their ideas and experiences, as Christian notions of marriage and sexual relationships are shaped anew for the twenty-first century.[14]

Friendship

There is a long tradition of positive writing about friendship within Christianity.[15] The importance of friendship has been honoured, just as Jesus honoured his friends, the male and female disciples. At particular moments, according to the Church's teaching on marriage and prevailing social attitudes to marriage, friendship has had particular significance – especially in the context of same-sex communities. This is a broad topic and for the purposes of this short essay, three brief examples have been chosen for the questions they raise about the history of marriage and sexuality.

The Middle Ages, a period in which it was required that priests be celibate, and in which monastic life (which also required celibacy) was thriving, saw the development of a strong literature on friendship. This should not surprise us. Once men and women were living in same-sex monastic communities, it was inevitable that questions about the living out of God's love in relationship to one another would be raised. Perhaps the most important treatise on friendship in this period was Aelred of Riveaux's *On Spiritual Friendship*. Aelred, as a twelfth-century Cistercian, was from a monastic order that especially emphasised an affective (or 'emotional') piety and initiated a great spiritual renewal. For Aelred, friendship had its origins in God's creative activity: the loving creator God brings together his creatures in society to unite them. Friendship therefore has spiritual significance, and is a way in which human beings share in the life of God. In a famous passage from the treatise, friendship is likened to charity or love, so that 'he that abides in friendship abides in God, and God in him.'[16] Aelred is saying: whoever knows deep friendship with another human being knows and reflects the love of God. At a time when celibacy was still considered the higher good, and monastic life was thriving, friendship – usually configured as between two people of the same sex – was given spiritual significance. How much this related to larger kinship networks, which were important at the time, or even same-sex sexual desire, has been much discussed by historians and we shall return to this in the section on homosexuality. Nevertheless, it is important to note that one of the reasons Aelred's ideas made such an impact was that he extended his concept of spiritual friendship to relationships between men and women. This remained unusual not only in his own medieval culture but even into the early modern (Reformation) period, where – despite the Protestant reformers' advocacy of marriage – primary relationships were still often between men and men, and women and women, even in the wider society as our next example illustrates.

Our second example does not concern particular Christian writings about friendship, but rather the continued importance of same-sex friendship networks even after marriage was given greater status in the Church's teachings. As we have seen, the Protestant Reformation in the sixteenth century initiated a sweeping change in Christian attitudes to marriage, and the reformers developed sophisticated theologies of marriage. However, the Protestant reformers' teaching about marriage and the household was, of course, just that – their teaching, not always the lived reality. Interestingly, then, historians of the Reformation period have pointed to the fact that 'Couples were as exceptional in the sixteenth and seventeenth centuries as they are common today. Men married in their late twenties, women in their mid-twenties, and, because adult mortality was so high, the married couple's average duration was less than twenty years.' In this period, the term 'couple' referred distinctly to married people, who made up only just over a third of the total British population and 'who occupied a status sharply distinguished from that of single folk, whose world can best be described as homosocial.'[17] The term 'homosocial' simply means that people of the same sex will tend to socialise and form close bonds with each other, sometimes (or often) to the exclusion of the opposite sex. Therefore, in sixteenth- and seventeenth-century European and British culture, which was still overwhelmingly rural, in feasts, dances and much of the other regular socialising which made up the rhythm of a village's year, boys and men tended to mix with each other more than with girls and women, and friendship was a vitally important bond carrying considerable social and emotional significance. The historian John Gillis points out that in our age 'we expect adolescent boys to gang together, . . . we encourage them to abandon those bonds as early as possible. In fact we rely on interest in the opposite sex to pry the young loose from their earlier camaraderie.' Thus, he suggests,

> Those who believe the conjugal bond to be the only possible relationship capable of fulfilling the human need for

companionship, intimacy, and love will find the homosocial world of the sixteenth and seventeenth century bizarre, even repelling. However, when we impose our own values on the past, we not only distort it but limit our ability to understand ourselves. As we turn to the sixteenth and seventeenth centuries it is well to keep in mind that it is not the capacity for love but the forms of affection that separates their world from ours.[18]

All of this means that nearly two-thirds of the population of Britain at any one time in this period were in an unmarried state. This is just one example – many could be given – to remind us that another age's understanding and practice of marriage and friendship may be quite different from our own; moreover, this should not surprise us for their context was profoundly different from ours.

Our third example comes from the writings of a woman, one of the rare examples in the Christian tradition of a woman offering teaching on marriage and friendship. Mary Astell was writing in late seventeenth- and early eighteenth-century England: well educated, well connected and a high Anglican, she wrote in 1696 *A Serious Proposal to the Ladies*, in which she suggested that single women should have a monastery or 'religious retirement' where they could develop their spiritual life and increase their intellectual learning. Astell was addressing a particular problem that had existed since the Protestant Reformation and the abolition of the nunneries. For pious Protestant women, it seemed that only one vocation remained – marriage – so where were 'spare' single women to go? Moreover, the Reformation had changed the perception of unmarried women: celibacy and holy virginity were no longer prized in Protestant culture. At the heart of Astell's proposal were: a belief that women too have souls and the faculty of reasoning, and should develop them; a desire to cultivate piety in the high Anglican manner, observing the feasts and fasts of the church in community; and a strong advocacy of female friendship. The proposal was directed at the educated, the 'middling and upper sorts' who had some financial means and the possibility of choice in their lives. She called for those who supported her to provide the money for such an enterprise, and pious

71

ladies came forward to do so. But the idea was squashed by leading churchmen who thought it too 'papist' and therefore dangerous. Astell, an unmarried and educated woman, in proposing such a 'monastery', highlighted the uncertain place of women in society if they *remained* unmarried. (It is worth note that convents were not revived in England until the mid nineteenth century when the Anglo-Catholics revived monastic life in the Church of England.) While Astell's proposal is one of the most well known, the historian Bridget Hill has demonstrated both that the idea of a Protestant nunnery persistently recurred in England from the sixteenth to the nineteenth century, and that the late seventeenth century, when Astell was writing, saw a particular 'surplus' of single women which made the question particularly acute.[19] In those circumstances, female friendship was especially important in forming a supportive network. Friendship was vital to women such as Astell for life alone could be lonely: in the dedication of her 1689 *Collection of Poems* to the Archbishop of Canterbury, she describes herself as a single woman, newly arrived in London, with 'none that careth for her soul, even when my kinsfolk had failed, and my familiar friends had forgotten me'.[20] To survive she needed friends, and she became part of a circle of pious and intellectual women with whom she enjoyed companionship, mental stimulation and bonds of affection.

People need the intimacy of friendship and for different reasons: because they live in community or because they are single or because – most importantly – in friendship as in marriage we experience and reflect God's love in companionship with one another. In our own age, the Church has been so keen to shore up marriage in the face of changing societal patterns, that it has often forgotten not only the importance of friendship, but also its godly nature.

Homosexuality

It may seem somewhat odd to end this essay with only a relatively short section about homosexuality, when clearly the raison d'etre for this book is the disagreement within the churches today about homosexuality. There are two reasons why this section comes last. First, same-sex relationships are often compared (and usually unfavourably) with 'traditional' marriage. One of the purposes of this essay has been to show that the Church has regarded marriage in a variety of ways throughout two thousand years of Christian history. Furthermore, the nature of marriage and family life has necessarily changed, and the Church has adapted its ideas to changing social and economic conditions. There is no fixed and unchanging notion of 'marriage' in the Christian tradition to which we can easily compare contemporary homosexual relationships. Secondly, homosexuality as we understand it today, as an identity – something that one *is* or *isn't* – is, according to most historians, a relatively modern concept, just as heterosexuality as an identity is also a modern idea. It is in the modern world that sexuality moved into the private sphere, and became increasingly a part of a person's identity, for which they were responsible. This is well illustrated by Rousseau in his *Confessions* (published in the 1780s) where he describes his sexual activities not merely as activities, but as strong indicators of his *character*. Only in 1869 was the term 'homosexuality' first coined (by the Swede, Hans Benkert), and it was not used in English until the early 1890s. Then it was largely used in medical circles where homosexuality became the object of scientific investigation and pathologisation.

This is not to say that sexual activity between two people of the same sex did not take place before the modern period! But all sexual activity – whether between men and women, men and men or women and women – was regarded as just that: *activity*. And, of course, some activities became illegal: in the 1530s, as the Protestant Reformation was getting going, sodomy was made a capital crime in England and in the Holy Roman Empire. Sodomy, like the activity of prostitution, with which it was often linked and which was also clamped down on in this period, was considered threatening to marriage. Despite this, the number of sodomy cases in the sixteenth and seventeenth centuries remained quite small, and the activity was not at that time connected with any particular sub-culture. As Diarmaid MacCulloch has put it,

> There was no descriptive term at all in the prescriptive litera-
> ture for the notion of a homosexual identity; sodomy was a
> matter of corrupted individuals making choices to carry out
> certain acts. All people could fall, and the consequences were
> dire, not just for the individual but for all society . . . Therefore
> sodomy was linked to any group which could be represented as
> threatening the structure of society.[21]

This takes us back to the nature of the household in the
Reformation period: it was a unit of society – 'a little commonwealth' – and if there was disorder in the household
then it could spread disorder to the nation; behaviour that
we would consider 'private' was (then) nothing of the sort.

MacCulloch goes on to argue, as do many other historians, that it was only in the late seventeenth century at the
earliest, and into the eighteenth century, that 'sub-cultures'
of 'homosexual' men began to gather, first in Amsterdam
and London. That such an identity could begin to emerge
had everything to do with shifting ideas about gender in
society. As older Galenic ideas about man and woman
being 'one sex' on a hierarchical continuum declined, so
'male' and 'female' developed as distinctively different
identities, and there was a new notion of sexual or gender
difference (what Laqueur calls the two-sex model). The
notion of gender complementarity – the idea that male and
female are somehow *naturally* made for each other – likewise developed, and those who did not fit into that scheme
began to emerge with a different identity: the effeminate
man and the mannish woman, whose sexual desire lay
with those of the same sex.

It is, however, the view of some historians, most
famously John Boswell, a medieval historian, that we *can*
talk about homosexuality before the modern period. He
pointed to the many examples of affection between men in
biblical and other Christian texts, and argued that before
the thirteenth century, Christians did not regard male
desire for sexual activity with other men as strange or even
bad.[22] In many ways, this is all a question of interpretation
(just as it is with the 'touchstone' biblical texts about homosexuality). The example of Anselm is instructive. When he
wrote in a letter to one of his former pupils, Gilbert Crispin,

'but you know how great is the affection we have experienced – eye to eye, kiss to kiss, embrace to embrace' to what activity was he referring?[23] He certainly may not have been referring to sodomy, but it does not mean that his words did not speak to and of genuine same-sex desire. And should we, can we, even ask questions about 'homosexuality' – our questions – to and about a culture in which 'homosexual identity' did not exist?

Similar questions of interpretation have been raised by Boswell's claim in a later book[24] that there existed in the pre-modern period liturgical rites for the celebration of permanent non-monastic unions between two people of the same sex. Boswell discovered manuscripts of such a liturgical rite, in Greek, dating from the eighth to the seventeenth centuries. On publication of his book, which of course occurred in the context of today's churches debating whether to bless same-sex unions, there was much controversy about what these past rites meant. Since then, scholars have discovered further examples of such rites, from the Latin West.[25] The confusion arises when we think – whether with horror or pleasure – of such rites being 'like marriage' and imposing modern ideas of marriage and its rites back to a pre-modern world. For we need to remember that marriage rites were not fixed in the medieval and early modern periods; it was not therefore a case of making the bonds between two men or two women 'like marriage'. In the Middle Ages and even into the early modern period, forms of marriage were often haphazard and very much a part of folk culture. While the Church attempted to take control of marriage ceremonies and bring them into the Church, this was a slow process. More informal arrangements persisted in the large majority of the population: couples who lived together and had children were deemed to be married, and legally only the consent between the man and woman was required, without witnesses. In England, for example, the Book of Common Prayer provided a marriage service, and parishioners were urged to make use of this. However, it has been estimated that only about one-third of couples in the sixteenth and seventeenth centuries had their union blessed by a priest,[26] and it was only with Lord Hardwicke's Marriage Act in 1753 that all marriages legally had to take place within the Church of England. Furthermore, a rite for the making of 'brothers' or 'sisters', which is what Boswell discovered, had different meanings in a society where kinship ties were important and extended beyond what we envisage as 'family' and blood relations. People in the Middle Ages and early modern period were parts of much greater networks of household, kinship and friendship than we, in the modern West, usually experience or imagine. As historian Alan Bray has put it,

> The difficulty for the modern viewer lies in that modern society recognizes only one such 'voluntary' kinship, in marriage: in the past others have subsisted alongside it; and their aggregate effect was that (in England at least until well into the seventeenth century) an individual lived in effect in a potential plurality of families. He or she could be part of one family in terms of blood relations and simultaneously part of another in terms of the ritual kinship created by betrothal or marriage, by baptism or as here by 'sworn' brotherhood (or sisterhood).[27]

With homosexuality as with marriage, we have to be careful, therefore, not to impose our own presuppositions on the past.

Looking to the future

In this essay we have looked at the several paradigm shifts in the Church's thinking about marriage and celibacy, and – consequently – related issues such as friendship and sexuality. Many people would say that we are in the middle of another paradigm shift now – and it is painful! As we have seen before, the Church has both been proactive in radically changing its ideas about marriage and celibacy – most obviously in the Protestant Reformation – and has also adapted its teachings and maintained its dynamic sense of tradition in relationship to larger societal and cultural shifts. In our own day, at least in the West, marriage patterns are changing once again, with more divorces, more people living together before they marry (or instead of marrying), many children being raised happily in families in which the parents are not married, more people remaining single, and same-sex couples living openly together in stable, loving and monogamous relationships. So, for example, the Church has adapted its teaching on divorce and remarriage (despite Jesus' prohibition of divorce in the gospels) to be more accommodating to the broader culture's tolerance of divorce. For some Christians the sticking point is homosexuality; for other Christians there is no problem with full acceptance of same-sex relationships. Hence our disagreements.

What I have tried to suggest by the discussion in this essay is what we must *not* do. We must not impose back onto biblical texts and onto the Christian tradition, our own modern conception of what we think marriage is and always has been, and then use it as a stick with which to beat those who disagree with us. A lot of this goes on. When the creation story is invoked as the origin of 'traditional' marriage, it is time to be suspicious. When Adam and Eve are represented as 'complementary' to one another, sitting across the campfire from each other in domestic bliss (and it is amazing how many biblical commentaries and Christian texts evoke this fantastic idea) then it is important for us to remember that modern ideas about gender and marriage are being mapped back onto an extraordinarily different culture of several thousand years ago, and into a mental world which was quite different from ours. Or, to put it another way, that's an awful lot to load onto the text from Genesis, 'male and female he created them'. Many different views can be appealed to as 'traditional Christian teaching'. What the tradition primarily teaches us is that whatever the Church has taught as the 'ideal' at any moment in history, human beings are social creatures who, whether in sexual relationships, friendship or community, have sought to know and reflect God's love in companionship with one another. It is time to recognise that and pursue the work of forging a new paradigm which reads Scripture afresh for and in our times, just as our forefathers and foremothers did, and contribute to the development of the dynamic and living Christian tradition in which we live out our discipleship.

Notes

1 Diarmaid MacCulloch, *Reformation: Europe's house divided, 1490–1700* (London: Penguin, 2003), p.608.

2 See, as one example, *Some Issues in Human Sexuality: A guide to the debate* (London: Church House Publishing, 2003), paragraph 1.2.1, p.8.

3 Peter Coleman, *Christian Attitudes to Marriage* (London: SCM Press, 2004), p.99.

4 Wayne Meeks, *The Origins of Christian Morality: The first two centuries* (New Haven: Yale University Press, 1993), p.54.

5 Peter Brown, *The Body and Society: Men, women and sexual renunciation in Early Christianity* (New York: Columbia University Press, 1988), p.133.

6 Clarissa Atkinson, 'Precious Balsam in a Fragile Glass: The ideology of virginity in the late Middle Ages', *Journal of Family History* Vol. 8, No. 2, Summer 1983, p.133. Atkinson goes on to argue that this moral definition of virginity prevailed in the later Middle Ages 'because of the experience and reputations of the late medieval saints'.

7 'Statutes of the Realm' iv. Part I, p.67 in W. J. Sheils, *The English Reformation*, pp.94-5.

8 Lyndal Roper, *The Holy Household: Women and morals in Reformation Augsburg* (Oxford: Clarendon Press, 1989).

9 Thomas W. Laqueur, *Making Sex: Body and gender from the Greeks to Freud* (Cambridge, MA: Harvard University Press, 1990).

10 For an excellent discussion of this development see Leonore Davidoff and Catherine Hall, *Family Fortunes: Men and women of the English middle classes, 1780–1850* (London: Hutchinson, 1987).

11 Quoted in *Women in English Religion 1700–1925* ed. Dale A. Johnson (New York: Edwin Mellen Press, 1983). pp.129, 130, 131.

12 Resolution 41, Lambeth Conference 1908. *The Six Lambeth Conferences 1867–1920* (London: SPCK, 1929), p.327.

13 Henry Chadwick, *Augustine: A very short introduction* (Oxford: Oxford University Press, 1986), pp. 93-4.

14 A significant book here is Alison Webster, *Found Wanting: Women, Christianity and sexuality* (London: Cassell, 1995). She is particularly critical of the damaging effects of the idea of gender 'complementarity' on women.

15 For a survey of Christian ideas about friendship, see Liz Carmichael, *Friendship: Interpreting Christian love* (London: T & T Clark, 2004).

16 Aelred of Rievaulx, *Spiritual Friendship* (Washington DC: Cistercian Publications, Consortium Press, 1974), p.66.

17 John Gillis, *For Better, For Worse: British marriages, 1600 to the present* (Oxford: Oxford University Press, 1985), p.11.

18 ibid. pp. 35, 12.

19 Bridget Hill, 'A Refuge from Men: The idea of a Protestant nunnery', *Past and Present* No. 117, 1987, pp.107-130.

20 Quoted in Bridget Hill, *Women Alone: Spinsters in England 1660–1850* (New Haven and London: Yale University Press, 2001), p.163.

21 MacCulloch, *Reformation*, pp. 622-3.

22 John Boswell, *Christianity, Social Tolerance and Homosexuality* (Chicago: Chicago University Press, 1980).
23 St Anselm, 'Epistle 130' quoted in R. W. Southern, *Saint Anselm: A portrait in a landscape* (Cambridge: Cambridge University Press, 1990), pp.145-6.
24 John Boswell, *Same-sex Unions in Pre-Modern Europe* (New York: Villard Books, 1994).
25 See Alan Bray, 'Friendship, the Family and Liturgy: A rite for blessing friendship in traditional Christianity', *Theology and Sexuality* No. 13, September 2000, pp.15-33.
26 Lawrence Stone, *The Family, Sex and Marriage 1500–1800* (London: Penguin, 1989).
27 Bray, 'Friendship, the Family and Liturgy', p.27.

5 The Church and human sexuality: bringing a human rights perspective

Margaret Bedggood

All human beings are born free and equal in dignity and rights. They are endowed with reason and conscience and should act towards one another in a spirit of brotherhood.[1]

The purpose of this essay is to offer to the current debate on human sexuality within the Church a different perspective on human flourishing, a perspective derived from the theory, practice and experience of the modern human rights movement. If, as other writers in this collection contend, it is sensible or indeed often proper for Christians not only to take account of but even to profit from the learnings of science, biology and ethics, so might they similarly learn from and perhaps offer something in return to the law and social ethics of human rights, particularly as these relate to such fundamental Christian concepts as the nature of what it means to be human and the imperative to social justice.

The discourse of 'human rights' is not, generally, one with which the Church engages. Accordingly, this essay first outlines what is meant by human rights and emphasises its core values as a context for a perspective on human sexuality. It also addresses briefly some of the reasons for the Church's lack of engagement and seeks to remove some misconceptions which may contribute to it. The human rights discussion is then drawn back to parallels with underlying Christian principles and to ways in which past and current experience on issues of human sexuality might be shared to their mutual benefit.

Christian thinkers have not in general employed the modern language of human rights to aid biblical interpretation or the development and elucidation of doctrine and values. This is somewhat surprising, given the similarity of such core concepts as the essential value of being human – in the Christian context enhanced, or explained, by the incarnation and the creation of humankind 'in the image of God' – and the resulting call to social justice. Much of this rejection is founded on misconceptions or misinterpretations of what is meant by human rights, its origins and intentions, both in general and also particularly in the context of human sexuality.

Some of the reasons for this lack of engagement are explored below, but whatever they may be, this rejection has deprived the Church of a helpful resource, painfully and carefully developed through the last fifty years, which can provide content and insight for Christian social thinking and action at the beginning of the twenty-first century. So while it is not suggested that human rights theory is definitive or normative for Christians, as a significant modern social and legal movement it does form part of the historical development, and has informed our present day understanding, of many social justice issues. These are issues of the restoration of righteousness, if justice might be so described, with which the Church must grapple, if it is to remain true to the Gospel, and to its traditional way of working at doctrine, which has often been to incorporate gradually the learnings of what might be called 'secular revelation'.

What do we mean by 'human rights'?

To advance this task, and since the concept, content and aim of 'human rights' are all routinely criticised by theologians and religious adherents, some definition seems needed here. Also, two particular criticisms which are levelled at this modern concept of 'human rights' (and not, of course, only by theologians) need addressing. The first is that rights are too 'individualistic', and that far from being 'universal' they are in fact, culturally, and especially 'western' specific. Another criticism more commonly heard since the development of the 'war on terror' is that human rights have become too all-encompassing and are in danger of becoming therefore vague and unenforceable. This criticism may be advanced by theologians, perhaps fearing a 'secular religion', but more often by some human rights theorists themselves, who see the possibility of losing the core (as they see it) civil and political rights so hardly won.

'Human rights' in this essay means the corpus of human rights developed as international law since 1948, enshrined in the Universal Declaration of Human Rights and the two main covenants which brought that Declaration into a legal framework, and those rights as developed in the subsequent group- and issue-specific covenants and conventions, for example on torture, women, race and children.[2] These include both civil and political rights, such as freedom from torture, the right to a fair trial, to freedom of association and assembly; and economic, social and cultural rights, such as the right to education, to health, social security, housing, food and language. For historical and political reasons in the West and because of the effect of contemporary, that is twentieth-century, politics, in particular the Cold War, the original emphasis as far as development and implementation was concerned was on civil and political rights. But the need for a similar implementation and for the justiciability of economic and social rights has been increasingly recognised, and the indivisibility of all rights was affirmed in 1993 at the Vienna World Conference on Human Rights.[3] At that same conference emphasis was placed on the importance of the implementation of human rights 'on the ground', in domestic legal systems and increasingly in regional mechanisms.

It has also increasingly been recognised that sometimes, in order to be meaningful, rights and their observance must adhere to groups as well as individuals, to indigenous people, for example, or cultural minorities, and even, by extension in, for example, the right to development, to poorer states as against richer ones. Here we are entering a more controversial area, the whole question of international distributive justice, summed up by one writer thus:

> The idea of economic and social rights as human rights expresses the moral intuition that, in a world rich in resources and the accumulation of human knowledge, everyone ought to

be guaranteed the basic means for sustaining life, and that those denied these are victims of a fundamental injustice.[4]

One result of this legal framework established through the United Nations has been a partial surrender of state sovereignty. This may have been unintended at first and is still resisted or given reluctantly, but it is clear in, for example, such recent instances as the creation of the International Criminal Court and the growing acceptance of the concept of universal jurisdiction.

This legal framework is supported by, or merged with, a 'moral recognition' or framework of rights: that human beings have rights by virtue solely of being human; that having rights does not always mean exercising them; that rights imply responsibilities and obligations, either on the part of other individuals or of larger entities and organs of society, such as states, most commonly, or, increasingly, companies and other non-state actors (the duty-holders). And thus that individual rights exist within a network of obligations, both individual and collective, and of community connection.

The development of this legal and theoretical framework has also been accompanied by a growing movement of human rights activists whose task it is to see to it that rights are given actuality on the ground. Here the emphasis is not on a theoretical framework or legal treaties or moral imperatives, but on the recognition in all circumstances of human dignity and human worth; on the needs of victims, individuals, groups, and whole societies, in the face of gross violations of human rights in peace and war; on keeping governments and other actors honest; on giving voice to those who have no voice and empowering them to find their own.

Some questions about human rights: origins, universality, indivisibility, balancing

Modern human rights did not of course spring new into being in 1948; its origins and many of its values can be found in religious and philosophical traditions, including Christianity, and in the recent political history of western

83

Europe, in the women's movement, and in the labour rights which developed from the industrial revolution. It is noteworthy that when the Universal Declaration of Human Rights was being considered the drafters attempted to involve input from many traditions – philosophical, political and religious – from many parts of the world in order to gain that consensus which alone gives respect for human rights its legitimacy.

For that legitimacy depends on human rights universally attaching to all human beings. It is that universal applicability which is challenged often by non-western nations who allege that the current human rights norms are western derived and focused and are incompatible with their own cultures, religions or value systems. Certainly allowance must be made for cultural context, a 'margin of appreciation',[5] particularly in local implementation methods. But it is often worth asking who are the proponents of a more extreme cultural relativism, for it tends *not* to be those groups which are poor and marginalised in any society.

Another challenge to human rights concerns a matter of priority. Thus it is still argued that civil and political rights are of greater importance than economic, social and cultural rights. At a time like the present in the 'war on terror', when civil and political rights are unexpectedly under so much attack even in the countries where they have hitherto been most observed, it seems more than ever necessary to affirm their importance. But nevertheless this should not be at the expense of economic and social rights. President Franklin Roosevelt in his 'four freedoms' speech[6] recognised that these different rights must be indivisible so that freedom of speech and expression, freedom of everyone to worship God in his or her own way, freedom from want and freedom from fear must exist together, and so it was affirmed at the Vienna World Conference on Human Rights in 1993.

Another difficulty often seized on by critics of human rights including those in the Church is that presented by the necessity of balancing one right against another. How can a right to freedom of expression be reconciled with a prohibition against hate-speech? The rights of a woman against that of a child? The rights of a member of a group against the rights of that group as a whole? The rights of one group in society against those of the majority of that society and its values? In truth, the practice of human rights almost always calls for such balancing, for a process of discernment and consideration of the circumstances of each individual situation. In fact, casting a problem, whether political, social or religious, in terms of the rights of those involved, that is, taking a rights-based approach, may often assist rather than hinder the decision-making. What is required is courteous dialogue in the discernment towards balance, a recognition that no position can be absolute and that much may be gained and learned by thoughtful engagement.

From this account then it should be clear that the concept of 'human rights' extends beyond its legal recognition in international instruments or domestic legislation. It includes also the fundamental principles and values which underpin those legal norms, and which those norms recognise or admit but which they do not create. Thus this can be called a value system or even a belief system though not a theology or a religion. It may well be the closeness of this value system to that of Christianity which makes the Church wary of or openly antagonistic to human rights, an issue we will consider below. For now, let us turn to the core value or principle of human rights, and its relevance to human sexuality.

A core value: 'all human beings are born free and equal in dignity and rights'

Here in Article 1 of the Universal Declaration of Human Rights, at the heart of human rights theory and practice, lies its core value, the recognition of the dignity and worth of all human beings, *simply because they are human*. Regardless of the reasons why, the human rights community views the human person as inviolable or 'sacred',[7] entitled to basic rights of physical integrity and means of sustenance: that is the opportunity to lead a good life, even if that is undefined. That focus works in two ways: for the person it brings a sense of empowerment – the powerful, whether individual or collective, for example the state or the Church, have no monopoly on rights; and, contrary to what some critics of human rights allege, equally powerfully it brings a sense of responsibility for the rights of *others*. In particular, it is never acceptable to use people as things or to breach their rights as a means to any end, however laudable that end might be, unless they choose that course for themselves. Even the differences which are obvious between human beings are to be valued and 'magnified',[8] as part of that core identity, our essential humanity.

The language used to describe this core value is admittedly not uncontroversial and has been changed and challenged over time: equality, dignity, freedom, personhood, equal worth, anti-discrimination, have all been used to express this fundamental focus. Nor is it easy to articulate an underlying reason or justification for this principle, a point which theologians are quick to make. In the end, it may be only in and through specific practical examples that its justification can be seen.

Historically, the focus of the human rights campaign to recognise essential human-ness has been on preventing discrimination in relation to rights against particular groups, or rather against individuals by reason only of their belonging to a particular group. Thus the two main human rights covenants, on economic, social and cultural rights and on civil and political rights, contain one similar clause: both Article 2.1 of the International Covenant on Civil and Political Rights and Article 2.2 of the International Covenant on Economic, Social and Cultural Rights refer to rights being guaranteed or ensured 'without distinction (discrimination) of any kind, such as (as to) race, colour, sex, language, religion, political or other opinion, national or social origin, property, birth *or other status.*' (emphasis added)

From the earlier recognised grounds such as race and sex and their particular conventions[9] the concept of anti-discrimination has been extended to include, for example, age and disability. And it is clear that such extension was envisaged, through the addition of 'or other status', the balance between certainty, the affirmation of what we know now, and flexibility, leaving room for what we may learn in the future, being as important in the study of human rights as it is in biblical revelation. (The extension to sexual orientation – or sexual preference or sexuality or gender identity – at national and international level is discussed below.) This same core value, the recognition of essential human worth, is reflected also in efforts to protect other marginalised groups, such as immigrant workers, indigenous peoples and refugees.[10]

As the human rights movement has developed and become more established there has also been a move away from the desirability of homogeneity characteristic of the era of new nation building to increased recognition of the value of diversity. For denial of individual human dignity, the perception of another as less than human, has always led easily and inevitably to violations of their other rights, even to torture and death. History, including recent twentieth-century history, is full of examples of such identity-based violations, both on a huge scale as in Kosovo, Ruanda, Darfur, and in continued persecution of particular groups in all societies. And NGOs like Amnesty International continue to document them.[11] Thus it must be acknowledged that the legal recognition of equality can never be enough; other changes at individual, collective and national levels are required. At least legal recognition gives legitimacy and thus an impetus to such other more fundamental societal changes. Work for those other attitudinal changes is also a task for human rights – and for the Church.

Human sexuality in the context of human rights

Those same core values outlined above can be found in the history of the human rights movement's engagement with questions of human sexuality, even though, like the societies it reflects, it has come to them more recently and often it seems equally reluctantly. Women and gays, lesbians and bisexual and transgendered people have been in the history of our cultures and churches among the most disadvantaged and vilified groups, with the result that they have endured horrific violations of the most basic

87

human rights – and, in many societies in which the Anglican Church operates, still do; it is on women and gays that the burden of the denial of the right to full human personality, including the acknowledgement of sexuality, has fallen.

As the human rights movement has developed and come to understand better the indivisibility of all rights, physical, mental and spiritual, and the intersectionality of the discrimination of disadvantaged groups, so it has begun to acknowledge the rights inherent in human sexuality and to address violations of them. The Universal Declaration of Human Rights acknowledges such rights within its context of the traditional 'family' (Article 16); but gradually the discrimination borne by women and gays in this model has been recognised. For women this recognition has come at the international level, through the Convention on the Elimination of all forms of Discrimination against Women and the later Declaration on Violence against Women, through the work of the Committee on the Status of Women and the Special Rapporteur on Violence against Women and the recognition of rape and sexual violence as war crimes.[12] These approaches are now accepted more and more widely at the domestic level and increasingly the churches insofar as they continue to disadvantage women are seen to be out of step with the direction that societies, and not only societies in the West, are moving.

The history of the recognition of the rights of gays, lesbians, bisexual and transgendered people has been slower and is still far from universal. There has been acknowledgement at the level of the United Nations Treaty bodies, by the inclusion of sexual orientation (or sexual preference or sexuality) as another example of 'other status' in the Covenants and in some national jurisdictions in human rights statutes and occasionally in constitutions and by courts, as a ground on which discrimination is illegal. The Treaty bodies, such as the Human Rights Committee, have also frequently made the link to violations of other human rights resulting from discrimination in this context.[13]

But it must be acknowledged that this extension has not been recognised by the wider United Nations bodies where some states can effectively block such developments. At the recent (2004) session of the Commission on Human Rights, for example, some states, including the Vatican and Pakistan (representing the Organisation of Islamic Conference) were successful in having the resolution put forward by Brazil withdrawn. This resolution expressed 'deep concern' at the occurrence of human rights violations all over the world on grounds of sexual orientation and called on states and relevant UN human rights bodies to give due attention to these violations.[14]

In his report to the same meeting, the Special Rapporteur on the right to health developed the links between discrimination and the inability to enjoy sexual and reproductive health. This report was similarly severely criticised. But while formal recognition of these rights at this level has not yet been achieved, a growing number of non-governmental organisations and human rights defenders including from the Global South now appear regularly at United Nations forums – and the states in opposition appear to be becoming increasingly isolated and defensive.

Yet the arguments denying universality over issues of sexuality and sexual orientation continue to be strongly voiced. So it seems that in the context of sexual rights the anti-discrimination approach may not in fact be sufficient on its own: preferable may be a more positive claim to that common human identity of which sexuality is a core characteristic so that sexual rights are seen to apply to all, not just to sexual minorities. The Special Rapporteur in his Report to the Commission writes:[15]

> . . . sexuality is a characteristic of all human beings. It is a fundamental aspect of an individual's identity. It helps to define who a person is. The Special Rapporteur notes the abiding principles that have shaped international human rights law since 1945, including privacy, equality, and the integrity, autonomy, dignity and well-being of the individual . . . In these circumstances, the Special Rapporteur has no doubt that the correct understanding of fundamental human rights principles, as well as existing human rights norms, leads ineluctably to the recognition of sexual rights as human rights. Sexual rights include the right of all persons to express their sexual orientation, with

due regard for the well-being and rights of others, without fear
of persecution, denial of liberty or social interference.

Such an approach may also help to counter the argument
that homosexual orientation is only a western experience,
an argument which finds particular support in Church
discussions. This is a claim, endlessly repeated, which is
simply untrue: different sexual orientation has been evi-
dent in all historical periods and in all parts of the globe. It
is true that difficulties can arise because of the terms used
in western societies in the last century – such as 'sexual orientation' and 'gay and lesbian' – terms which may be
unworkable in societies which construct sexuality differ-
ently; but again this is a matter of the implementation and
interpretation of universality in a particular cultural
and societal context.

The Church's response to human rights

As mentioned in the introduction to this essay, the Church
has been slow to engage with the human rights movement.
There have been some theologians, and their number is
increasing, who have been prepared to draw helpful parallels with human rights thinking both in general terms or
with reference to specific issues, such as poverty or
inequality, and there are some scholarly works which treat
of these matters in depth.[16] But from the local pulpit or in
the local pew the use of human rights by way of support
for Christian belief or of example for Christian action
would still be rare. And very often the intention of any reference appears to be either co-option or refutation rather
than elucidation.

There seem to be a number of reactions or reasons which
fuel this reluctance. One of these, oddly enough, is to stress
the similarity of human rights precepts to Christian ones,
that very similarity which would make their citation helpful. And as we have seen, it is true that there are many similarities; one of the sources of the Universal Declaration of
Human Rights was assuredly Christian precepts, and some
early human rights battles were fought by Christian
thinkers and on biblical grounds, the abolition of slavery

for example. This would seem rather to be a reason for going further to see what else of later addition in the human rights canon might be useful in interpreting Scripture and tradition for twenty-first-century Christians.

More often, however, the discussion turns to centre on the admittedly difficult question of the basis of human rights: *why* should we think that human beings are equal simply because of their humanity, why respect the sacredness of that humanity and act towards them accordingly? Does not this equate to a belief system and/or require a belief in God to make sense of the sacredness? These are admittedly complex and as yet unresolved questions; questions which are theologically puzzling for Christians, and for Christian and other believing human rights activists in particular, and complex and puzzling for human rights activists who are not. For the latter, that is human rights activists whether Christian or not, this question has not proved paralysing. They have simply got on with putting the theory into practice. For theologians, however, it has too often proved a stumbling block. Either rights theory is seen as equivalent to, and derivative from, Christian thinking, in which case it has nothing to add, and/or it is viewed as inherently flawed for lack of a basis of any kind, let alone a theological one.

Perhaps the real difficulty is that human rights principles *are* too close to Christian principles in many ways, so that rights theory is seen as an alternative belief system and a dangerous one at that. It is therefore important to distance the Church from it and this over-rides any synergism which might have seen human rights as helpful for biblical interpretation and application. It is accordingly its negative aspects which must be emphasised. So there develops an opposition to 'rights' themselves, on the argument that it is God alone who has rights and to whom alone duties are owed. 'Rights' are equated with all that the Church, or sections of it, see as representing what is worst in the modern world, thus becoming a casualty of the tension between the 'world' and the Church which the Church so easily creates for itself. Thus 'rights' are deemed, in some parts of western churches, to be indicative of the permissive society and so, depending on what is seen as 'permissive', as too

individualistic or selfish, as encouraging resistance to legit-
imate authority, as promoting the interests of women, con-
tributing to the breakdown of traditional family values and
supporting sexual licence. In non-western parts of the
Church, rights talk is seen as particularly at odds with the
collective as opposed to the individual values of the society
and as such to be identified as part of western secularism
and as a new form of colonisation. When it comes to discussion of sexual rights, these oppositions and anxieties are
substantially increased, inevitably in an institution which
remains so deeply ambivalent about human sexuality.

This opposition to rights talk often then leads the Church
to lobby for and obtain exemption from any secular human
rights regime, pressing to the limits the extent to which the
law will allow this, as for example in the exemptions permitted by the UK Human Rights Act 1998.[17] Ironically such
call for exemption is often based on the claim to a fundamental right to freedom of religion which it is argued the
law should recognise and uphold. That the law of a society
which recognises such a right has moved on in that same
society to recognise other rights is a fact conveniently
ignored.

In the Anglican Communion are to be found all of
these reasons for reluctance or resistance, often with
groups coming together in unlikely alliance. Thus the lack
of a theological base, or of direct mention or correlation in
Scripture can be troubling to both the 'liberal' and 'evangelical' wings of the western Church; equality rights for
women or children are seen variously as unbiblical, selfish,
destructive of family values or local culture by some
Evangelicals and Anglo-Catholics and by Anglicans in
non-western cultures; and the emergence of 'sexual' rights
as deeply troubling on all these counts by part of the more
conservative section of the evangelical wing and many
non-westerners alike. In the Anglican Communion much
of this misconception may well be due to the influential
position exercised by, on the one hand, the Church of
England, the English having come late to the rights debate;
secondly by the Episcopal Church of the United States,
given the American overly litigious attitude to rights
which tends to fuel the accusation that rights exist without

corresponding duties; and thirdly by the growing numerical weight of the provinces in Africa and Asia.

A Gospel way forward on human sexuality

A comparison with the earlier outline of human rights theory will show that much of this Christian reluctance, ambivalence or opposition to employing the ideas and language of human rights can be attributed to misconception or misunderstanding or simply ignorance, or, to put it less kindly, misrepresentation of the tenets of human rights, and it can be seen that use is often made of the tactic of setting up a false image in order to demolish it, a tactic not unfamiliar in Christian argument. While historically there has been a number of issues on which the Church has been slow to embrace what has subsequently been seen as a Gospel position (slavery, apartheid, racial intolerance, the subjection of and violence against women), this essay is concerned particularly with its attitudes to gays and lesbians and to human sexuality more generally. From two points of view, that of the advancement of human rights on human sexuality and of the future of the Church, the response and record of the Church has been and continues to be a matter of deep concern. On this issue it has often been complicit in or has itself advocated discrimination and exclusion and the violence which inevitably results. And even when this is not so, the niceties of the theological or biblical distinctions which its adherents make are lost on those who see them only as supporting discrimination and thus licensing violence. Insistence on exclusion from the leadership of the Church on this ground alone suggests, as previously was the case with women, that the Church views gays and lesbians as somehow unfit compared with 'normal' people. And finally there is the question of blatant hypocrisy: in western churches the numbers of gay and lesbian priests are conveniently ignored, and in non-western churches other sins apparently biblically prohibited such as polygamy are not condemned. None of this does anything for the Church either in the eyes of many of its adherents, who are ashamed, or of those outside who are frankly derisive.

The comparison with previous positions taken towards women by the Anglican Church (and still taken by some sections of the wider Church) might prove instructive here. Paradoxically, the Church was drawn by secular developments including those in the human rights field, and by the involvement in those developments of Christian women, to a reappraisal of its own tradition and of scriptural interpretation and thus to a more inclusive position. In that context too, words like 'normal' and 'natural', or 'in accordance with nature', were used to define the paradigm, men, against which women were measured.

Perhaps this time, faced with the call for justice for another excluded group, the Church might take the opportunity to be in time to contribute to and help shape the secular dialogue. It appears that we are in the midst of a profound cultural change on matters of sexuality, where, as we have seen, the human rights movement, one of the influential players in the development of modern cultural expression, like other parts of civil society and governmental and intergovernmental organisations, is feeling its way. How then might the Church engage positively in this paradigm shift? Can it find any Gospel course to guide it here? In other crises of faith and conflict and collapse, the Church, its prophets and leaders have frequently resorted to an approach which might be called 'back to basics', to asking fundamental questions: What does God require of you? Or, as Christopher Rowland reminds us in his earlier essay, what would Jesus have done? And frequently this explanation has been assisted, not determined but aided and illuminated, by secular developments, by thinking outside the 'religious' box.

There are three intertwining themes in the biblical narrative, highlighted in Jesus' own life and teaching, which might be seen as relevant here, and in the modern interpretation and consideration of which the human rights tradition could have something to contribute. These three themes are the increasing acknowledgement that the all-embracing love of God demands an inclusiveness of all humanity; that such inclusiveness must lead to a call to social justice, broadly defined; and that central to the biblical revelation is a recognition of the Trinitarian importance of relationship.

The first of these, the all-embracing nature of God's love, is present as early as at least one strand of Exodus tradition and in Isaiah and the prophets, although often obscured by the apparent exclusiveness of the covenant relationship. But it becomes startlingly clear in the fact of the incarnation and in the teaching and actions of Jesus himself. In these he showed that this love extends to all human beings, however different in some respects, however apparently 'outside' the societal or cultural acceptable norm – the Samaritan woman at the well is one such example, but there are many others. Jesus' own growth in understanding here, as outlined in Matthew's account of the importunity of the Canaanite woman,[18] provides a fascinating insight into the process of incremental revelation. A similar development can be seen in Paul's acceptance of the Gentiles and in Francis of Assisi, one of the most attentive of his followers, in his encounters with the leper, a social outcast, and with the Sultan of Egypt, an enemy alien. The recognition of the dignity of difference and the value of human worth enlarges in these instances the theology of those who admit them.

In contrast, the Church's record since has been painfully exclusive: of foreigners, 'heretics', women, the poor, children, the mentally ill, the physically disabled, some races as compared with others, and those we would now call gays and lesbians. The exclusionary violence of the twentieth century which gave birth to the human rights movement has meant, as we have seen, that its core value has had to be an acceptance of universal humanity. The Church might thus, if it can recognise the Gospel path here, learn from the difficulties, mistakes, insights and forbearance which the human rights movement has painfully experienced and which are now being put to work in the service of gays and lesbians.

Linked closely to and indeed deriving directly from the theme of the inclusiveness of God's love is the imperative call to social justice, for inequity in the treatment of God's people either individually or structurally is incompatible with that love. Again, this requirement for social justice can be found in the Old Testament, in the Jubilee tradition and in the emphasis on caring for the poor, widows, orphans and strangers. And again it is picked up in Jesus' teaching and actions and extended in his advocacy of non-violence and by Francis' emphasis on poverty and on mediation and reconciliation.

In this regard, the Church's record has in some respects been more encouraging: in Catholic social teaching on work and poverty, in the history of Anglican and Methodist Christian socialism, and in Quaker teaching on peace and reconciliation. One could cite such Christian initiatives as the abolition of the slave trade, the spread of liberation theology, the Catholic Worker movement, Jubilee 2000, the WCC campaign to abolish the death penalty, and recent initiatives for fair trade or against HIV/AIDs. But in other respects the response here has been selective, in contradiction to the requirements of a God 'for whom there are no strangers'. The exclusion of any group, the condoning of hierarchies of justice between nations, the failure to work for peace, all these work against the Church's own call for social justice. As it struggles with everything from the just treatment of its own members to questions of global distributive justice, or to what is acceptable in war or how better to make and maintain peace, again the human rights movement has its mistakes and its experience to offer.

The search for global distributive justice may be helped by a rights-based approach including that of a right to development, as may the active working for peace. And as the Church begins to come to grips with the need to exist in a religiously pluralist society, both globally and locally, it may learn from the human rights techniques of courteous and open dialogue. In particular, as it seeks to apply the two underlying biblical themes in discerning the way forward in its treatment of gays and lesbians it might take notice of the way that an acceptance of the universality of non-discrimination has led the human rights movement to employ its own pointer in 'other status'; the recognition that the widening of inclusiveness has made the deliberate exclusion of one group even more problematic, especially when the events which precipitated the modern growth of human rights involved the violent persecution of that group alongside others; how addressing discrimination and violence against gays may lead to a broader view of the nature of human sexuality, one more in keeping with the flourishing of human personality.

The third of these linked themes is the unfolding of the biblical revelation of the importance of relationship, both as the ideal within the Trinitarian nature of God, and also at the heart of the relationship between God and humankind, and how that affects and is affected by our relationships with each other. Again, our gradual realisation can be traced through Old Testament covenant and commandment to Jesus' own descriptions of the nature of his and our relationship with God, and later in the images of such as Julian of Norwich or Anselm of Canterbury. But the Church has too often, as other essays have shown, concentrated on particular sexual expressions of relationship rather than on those relationships themselves or on broader concepts of sexuality. This may seem a long way from the Special Rapporteur's discussion of sexual rights as human rights.[19] But there too the human rights movement is beginning to recognise the need for a broader human rights context for a true understanding of sexuality. If we acknowledge how much sexuality, however expressed, lies at the heart of human relationships, and with F. D. Maurice[20] that: 'Human relationships . . . are actually the means, and the only means through which man ascends to any knowledge of the divine' then it is imperative that the Church persevere in its understanding of such relationships; and to that end be prepared to adopt insights from other sources which might assist in that task of deepening our understanding of biblical revelation. For ultimately it must be that revelation *together with* the culture through which we receive it, which gives us our theology, our knowledge of God.

Notes

1 Article 1 of the Universal Declaration of Human Rights, adopted by the UN General Assembly resolution 217A (III) on 10 December 1948.
2 International Covenant on Economic, Social and Cultural Rights, adopted 16 December 1966, entered into force 3 January 1976;

International Covenant on Civil and Political Rights, adopted 16 December 1966, entered into force 23 March 1976; International Convention on the Elimination of all forms of Racial Discrimination, adopted 21 December 1965, entered into force 4 January 1969; Convention on the Elimination of all forms of Discrimination against Women, adopted 18 December 1979, entered into force 3 September 1981; Convention against Torture and other Cruel, Inhuman or Degrading Treatment or Punishment, adopted 10 December 1984, entered into force 26 June 1987; Convention on the Rights of the Child, adopted 20 November 1989, entered into force 2 September 1990.

3 Vienna Declaration and Programme of Action (1993).

4 D. Beetham 'What Future for Economic and Social Rights?', *Political Studies 41* (1995), p.43.

5 Maastrich Guidelines on Violations of Economic, Social and Cultural Rights (see 20 HRQ (1998)), pp.691-705.

6 F. D. Roosevelt 'Four Freedoms' speech, State of the Union Address, 1941, quoted in R. Russell, 'A History of the United Nations Charter' (1958) Annex B.

7 See the discussion in M. J. Perry, *The Idea of Human Rights: Four inquiries* (OUP, 1998), Chapter 1.

8 See ACNS 3837: Rowan Williams' Sermon at the Shrine of Our Lady of Walsingham, 31 May 2004.

9 See note 2.

10 International Convention on the Protection of the Rights of all Migrant Workers and members of their families, adopted 18 December 1990, entered into force 1 July 2003; Convention Relating to the Status of Refugees, adopted 28 July 1951, entered into force 22 April 1954; and Protocol Relating to the Status of Refugees, entered into force 4 October 1967; Draft Declaration on the Rights of Indigenous Peoples (begun 1985).

11 See, for example, 'Honduras: Human rights violations against lesbian, gay, bisexual and transgender people', September 2003, AI: AMR 37/014/2003; 'Sudan: At the mercy of killers – destruction of villages in Darfur', AI: AFR 54/072/2004; 'Serbia and Montenegro (Kosovo/Kosova), the March Violence' AI: EUR 70/016/2004.

12 Declaration on the Elimination of Violence against Women (adopted 1993). Special Rapporteur on Violence against Women, established 1994.

13 Consideration of Reports Submitted by States Parties, United States of America, CCPR/C/79/Add. 50 (1995), para 287; Concluding Observations of the Human Rights Committee: Chile (1999), CCPR/C/79/Add. 104, para 20; Concluding Observations of the Human Rights Committee: Sudan, 19/11/97 CCPR/C/79/Add. 85; Concluding Observations of the Human Rights Committee: El Salvador, CCPR/CO/78/SLV (2003); Concluding Observations of the Human Rights Committee: Colombia, CCPR/C/79/Add. 76 (1997), para 16; Concluding Observations of the Committee against Torture: Czech Republic, 20/05/94, CAT/C/21/Add. 2, para 33; Concluding Observations of the Committee against Torture: Brazil, CAT/A/56/44

(2001), para 119; Concluding Observations of the Committee against Torture: Egypt, CAT/S/XXIX/Misc. 4 (2002), para 5(e).

14 Draft Resolution 'Human Rights and Sexual Orientation', E/CN.4/2003/L.92; see Decision 2003/118 of the 59th Session of the CHR, 25/4/03.

15 E/CN, 4/2004/49, para 54.

16 For example, recently C. D. Marshall, *Crowned with Glory and Honor* (Pandora Press: US, 2001); or, less recent, J. Moltmann, *On Human Dignity, Political Theology and Ethics* (SCM Press, 1984); K. Leech, *The Sky is Red: Discerning the signs of the times* (DLT, 1997). (There is also a substantial 2-volume academic work, ed. John Witte and Johan Van Der Vyver, *Religious Human Rights in Global Perspective*, Kluwer Law International, 1996.) Books on particular issues, for example, M. Taylor, *Poverty and Christianity* (SCM Press, 2000); A. E. Harvey, *Demanding Peace* (SCM Press, 1999); D. M. Forrester, *On Human Worth: A Christian vindication of equality* (SCM Press, 2001).

17 See P. W. Edge and G. Harvey, *Law and Religion in Contemporary Society: Communities, individuals and the state* (Ashgate, 2000), Chs 4, 8 and 9.

18 Matthew 15:22.

19 Above, p.89.

20 F. D. Maurice, *The Kingdom of Christ* (1838), III 288.

6 Human nature, Christian vocation and the sexes

Robert Merrihew Adams

It is widely believed that sexual intercourse between persons of the same sex is 'unnatural', or contrary to nature, and bad or wrong for that reason. This view has strongly influenced both theological and untheological thinking about human sexuality. I believe classification of types of sexual activity as unnatural deserves to be treated with extreme scepticism. I also believe that a better conceptual framework can be found for Christian ethical thinking about sexuality. My aim in this essay is to explain and defend the views I have just stated.

Is anything unnatural?

There is a simple and obvious objection to classifying as unnatural any type of behaviour that actually occurs. Homosexual activity is an obvious example. It does actually occur, probably in virtually all human societies. It occurs because people actually desire it, are physically able to engage in it, and often experience some satisfaction in doing so. Those facts can hardly be denied. Nor do they seem to involve anything *supernatural*. Why should we not conclude that homosexual activity occurs because it is *naturally* possible for some human beings to desire it and to engage in it? So what is unnatural about it?

That argument is too short to settle the matter. For it has been held that the natural and the supernatural are not the only alternatives here, that the unnatural is a third alternative. This might once have been claimed on the basis of the Aristotelian view that every living thing, such as a horse or a human being, has a *nature* which defines the *telos* or goal of that being's life, and which is an internal generative cause of tendencies and behaviour leading toward the goal, and typical of the species to which the individual belongs. On this view, if the operation of an individual's nature is obstructed by accident or by its own voluntary choices, resulting impulses and actions contrary to the nature can be criticised as unnatural. I will not dwell on this approach here. It still has a following in the Roman Catholic Church, but cannot be assumed as normative in other Churches. It is unlikely to seem plausible to most of us because its Aristotelian conception of natures is overwhelmingly rejected by modern philosophers and biologists.

According to typical modern conceptions of nature, everything that happens happens in accordance with natural laws, with the sole and debated exception of events due to supernatural intervention. This is not necessarily to say that everything that happens was strictly determined, for our science recognises statistical or probabilistic laws as well as deterministic ones. But if phenomena are governed by statistical laws, an event barely possible but extremely improbable according to the laws is no more *contrary* to the laws of nature than an event that is overwhelmingly probable. Improbable events can and do occur, and that's part of the basis for thinking of phenomena as governed by statistical laws. Even if we think of the laws as embodied in powers and dispositions of particular things, it is no part of modern natural science to discriminate, among the potentialities and tendencies of a thing, between some that are natural and some that are frustrations of nature. Anything a thing can do is as natural as anything else it can do.

From a modern biological point of view, a *species* is not defined by a fixed and unchanging 'nature' or set of properties, as in the Aristotelian conception, but is seen as a population of genealogically related individuals whose inherited genetic properties (grounded in their DNA) are markedly similar but also include a considerable range of diversity that changes from one generation to another. The dissimilarities of members of the species are as natural as their similarities. Scientifically regarded, an individual organism's departure, by random mutation, from the usual patterns of its ancestors is not unnatural or a 'monstrosity', but is an ordinary part of the normal and natural processes of development and renewal of life.

The biologist may, to be sure, think of some dispositions and types of behaviour as functional and others as dysfunctional. But what function is in view here? The one function most clearly suggested by modern biological theory is the propagation, not of species as such, but simply of whatever genes the individual happens to have. This biological goal could in principle be served (and in some species is served) by aggressive and even murderous competition as well as by co-operation. It does not offer a criterion of ethical value that will be plausible from a Christian point of view, or from most secular points of view.[1] For such reasons it seems to me unwise to expect to read ethical values off modern scientific accounts of the natures of things.

Here I must emphasise some things I am *not* denying. Some human actions and dispositions are good and others are bad. Some human sexual activities are far from innocent, rape being only the most obvious example. We are social beings and will be hampered in living well if we do not react as most other human beings do *in certain respects*. What I deny is that concepts of the natural and the unnatural are likely to help us distinguish rightly between good and bad in these matters.

To some readers the previous arguments may seem unconvincingly theoretical. They may think that without any assistance from Aristotelian ideas about biological teleology, they can judge for themselves that (for example) homosexual acts, and homosexual desires, 'just don't seem natural'. And it is true that we have untheoretical ways of expressing approval of something by saying that it seems 'natural', or disapproval by saying that it seems 'unnatural'. Commonly this expresses an unreasoned inclination for or against the thing in question, a sense that we could easily go for the thing that 'seems natural', and that it would be hard to force ourselves to go for the thing that 'seems unnatural'. I do not mean to deny such feelings and seemings a role in ethical thinking. But two cautionary comments about them are in order in the present context.

The first is that in saying in this way that something

seems unnatural to me, I may both express disapproval and specify more particularly the flavour of my disapproval, but I do not thereby give a *reason* for my disapproval, as I do not give a *reason* for thinking the thing unnatural. We are confronted here with a value judgement, an intuitive judgement, as philosophers might call it, presented not as a conclusion of argument, but as a datum, or perhaps a starting point for ethical reflection. That is not necessarily an objection, but I take it as a reminder that we need to focus here pretty directly on the question, what seems to us, in our experience of human life, to be good or bad.

The second, related comment is that in relying on such intuitive judgements we ought to be very much on our guard against the temptation of mistaking our own subjective likes and dislikes, our own needs and fears, for interpersonally valid perceptions of objective goodness and badness. I do believe there are such objective perceptions, but we cannot reasonably claim them without careful and self-critical reflection on our intuitions; and we should be pretty cautious about them if we have not discussed them as open-mindedly as we can manage with people whose views and experience of life are relevantly different from ours. My first reaction to the idea of eating a grasshopper was certainly that it would be a revolting thing to do; I think I would have found it 'natural' to say that it seemed an 'unnatural' thing to do – not something that would 'come naturally' to me. Even now I definitely hope that I will never have compelling reason to eat a grasshopper – fried, baked or even coated in chocolate. But I cannot seriously regard this reaction of mine as a perception of objective badness. For having followed my inclination, and never eaten a grasshopper, I don't know what they taste like. And I've heard a former student of mine, who was married to an anthropologist, tell of living for months in a society in which fried grasshoppers were generally prized as the most delicious of foods. It would be silly for me to condemn their diet as unnatural and bad, trusting my own inexperienced prejudice against their experience.

The application to the debate about homosexuality is obvious. If people who have little or no experience of homosexual practices feel that they seem unnatural and bad, they should reflect that many people who have much experience of such practices not only judge that they can be, and often are, good, but also feel that they are natural, fitting who they most deeply are. Arguably no one's intuitions can put a view on such an issue beyond criticism or argument; but if we are weighing intuitions, intuitions based on more experience seem to deserve more weight than intuitions based on less.

Living in a world in which we are confronted much more directly than our ancestors with wide diversities of human experience, human cultures, and possible ways of life for human beings, most of us are conscious of a need for generous tolerance and respect for diversity as an aspect of respect for other people. At the same time, for most of us, there are contexts in which human diversity is alarming. Such fears can be very harmful, but should not surprise us, for we are deeply invested in compatibility with other humans, and some similarities of predisposition are crucial for some of the most important and most highly valued aspects of human life. A human child brought up among speakers of English will learn to speak English, and the same child brought up among speakers of Chinese would learn to speak Chinese; but a young chimpanzee brought up by humans speaking either language would not acquire more than an extremely limited, fragmentary, and perhaps debatable use of any human language. For a human child not to have a predisposition to use language as it is used by other humans it meets is obviously a terrible affliction. Likewise we would not be able to reason with each other, or perhaps to reason at all, if we did not have similar predispositions with regard to the forms of argument we will accept as valid.

Still none of us thinks that all differences among humans are bad, or that very common human qualities are always better than rare ones. 'Perfect pitch', for example, is uncommon, but the musical perceptions of people who have it are more reliable than those that most of us have. Loving one's enemies is commended by Christ, but is hardly experienced as 'coming naturally' to most people. And the reported action of Francis of Assisi in kissing a leper is certainly unusual, and may on first thought seem intuitively quite 'unnatural', but is widely (and I think rightly) regarded as saintly. With regard both to unusual and to prevalent types of behaviour and disposition, we need reflective and critical, and where possible reasoned, ways of distinguishing the good from the bad; and the mere fact that something is exceptional or typical in human beings is of little use as a basis for that discernment.

Creation and the vocation of the sexes

If we are trying to think about these issues in a context of Christian ethics, we will want a theological framework for our attempts to discern what is good and bad. Many have sought such a framework for Christian sexual ethics in a doctrine of creation. Some would make room for the category of the unnatural by combining the idea of creation with that of a 'fall' from the original perfection of the creation, a fall brought about by sins of human beings, and perhaps even earlier of angels. In such a framework it can be claimed that the actuality that is now available for our empirical observation is not nature as it came from the hand of its creator, but a *fallen* nature. In it not everything is truly natural that actually occurs and that may even be predicted by practitioners of the 'natural', or at any rate empirical, sciences, but some of those things are *unnatural* in the sense of not conforming to the original purposes of the creator.

The soundness of the conception of a historical 'fall' of humanity that is affirmed in such theologies is controversial among Christians, but it is not necessary to debate it here. For distinguishing as suggested between what is natural and what is empirically actual breaks the epistemological teeth of the idea of the unnatural. How are we to know that something that actually happens often enough is contrary to an original purpose of the creator, and thus unnatural? Both heterosexual marriage and homosexual behaviour as actually experienced take place, presumably, within the context of fallen humanity. What is to distinguish one as natural and the other as unnatural? So far as I can see, the idea of a fallen humanity provides no basis for making such a distinction without already *presupposing* that one of the types of behaviour is bad, wrong or contrary to a divine purpose or command. For such reasons I believe that in doing ethics, even in the context of a doctrine of creation, it will be best to set aside the distinction between natural and unnatural, and focus directly on the types of ethical or theological judgement that would be presupposed in making the distinction.

The obvious question to ask at this point, if our treatment of sexual ethics is to be part of a theology of creation, is whether a relevant purpose of the creator, opposed to homosexual behaviour, can be discerned even from our present empirically observable, and fallen, condition, or from the testimony of Holy Scripture. I go first to the question of purposes rather than commands, because I do not believe that unrationalised or apparently arbitrary commands have a secure place in Christian ethics, even if they appear to be endorsed in places by biblical writers. Orthodox Jews sometimes say that they do not need to know why God has forbidden Jews to eat pork or to work on Saturdays – that the commandments may have been given to Israel by God's grace simply in order to provide them with a way of expressing their devotion to God through obedience. The faithfulness that comes to expression in that view claims our deep respect, but I do not think it fits the specific character of Christian ethics.

Jesus is reported to have shocked some of his co-religionists by letting his teaching on divine commandments be guided by views of the divine purposes and human goods to be served by obedience, saying famously, for instance, that 'the Sabbath was made for the human being, and not the human being for the Sabbath' (Mark 2:27). Paul points in the same direction, inviting the Corinthian Christians to focus not on what they've been told to do but on the divine purpose to be fulfilled, when he accepts the saying, 'All things are permitted for me, but not all things are helpful' (1 Corinthians 6:12). I doubt that Paul invariably manages to take up this invitation in his own thinking, but surely it fits his emphasis on the freedom of a Christian and the fulfilment of the divine law by love (Galatians 5:13-14). And it is what we should expect if Christian life is to be life in the

Spirit in a new covenant in which the crucial inscription of God's law is in our hearts (Jeremiah 31:31-34), and in which Jesus says to his disciples, 'No longer do I call you slaves, for the slave does not know what his master is doing; but I have called you friends, for all that I have heard from my Father I have made known to you' (John 15:15). Any sensible ethics will recognise times when it is wise to be guided by the advice of people who know more than we do, but Christian ethics is not to be in the last analysis the obedience of slaves who do not know the divine purpose that makes sense of the duties they recognise.

What purposes of our creator, then, can we discern regarding human sexuality? We may begin, as many have, with the first two chapters of Genesis. Two divine purposes for sexuality are pretty clearly suggested there. Immediately after telling us that God created the human being male and female, the first chapter tells us that God commanded them to 'Be fruitful and multiply, and fill the earth' (Genesis 1:28). We can hardly fail to see here an implication that God intends human sexuality to play a part in the propagation of the human race – nor would anyone with much knowledge of human life find it hard to believe that if God has any purposes for human sexuality, one divine purpose for sexual intercourse is its procreative effect. And homosexual intercourse obviously cannot accomplish that procreative effect.

Does this imply or suggest that God forbids or disapproves of homosexual intercourse? Let us suppose, for the sake of argument (though I think it will not seem a plausible hypothesis in the end), that the procreative effect was God's sole original purpose in equipping humans for sexual intercourse. The ethical question most obviously invited by that supposition is why we should infer from it any condemnation of acts in which people use sexual intercourse for other purposes. Consider a couple of analogies. What purpose may God have had in creating the human *nose*? The likeliest answer is that the nose is for breathing and olfactory perception. But many of us also use our noses to prop up our eyeglasses, and no one condemns us for oculistic perversion of the nose! The tongue, likewise, obviously functions in eating and speaking, and participates in the noblest offices of religious speech. But will anyone claim with a straight face that it is a perversion, or even just wrong, for a clown to use her tongue to entertain children by trying to touch it to the tip of her nose?

I anticipate the reply that what is objectionable about homosexual intercourse is not simply that it is using human sexual organs for a *different* purpose from that which God originally intended, but that it is using them in a way that *frustrates* their procreative function. This is a very unpersuasive argument. First of all it is obvious that procreation is not prevented by homosexual acts as such. It may be prevented by homosexuals' abstinence from heterosexual intercourse, but is equally prevented by such abstinence on the part of celibate heterosexuals. I anticipate the reply that the homosexuals are frustrating the procreative function of their sexuality by a pattern of *using* as well as not using it, whereas the heterosexual celibates are simply *not* using their sexuality. But it is not obvious how this difference is relevant to our ethical evaluation, and it is also not obvious that celibates who conceive of themselves as offering their sexuality to God are not in that way *using* it. Moreover, homosexual people, as well as heterosexual people, now can and sometimes do participate in procreation through artificial insemination – not to mention that there are bisexual people who may engage in homosexual intercourse and also procreate through heterosexual intercourse. Finally, in a world now populated by about six billion people, it seems pretty clear that neither homosexuals nor celibates today have much reason to fear that God's procreative purpose for humanity will fail of fulfilment for lack of their participation.

It is a question worth asking why it should ever have been thought that the obviously plausible view that God has a procreative purpose for human sexual intercourse would imply a divine prohibition of non-procreative forms of sexual intercourse. I do not see a breath of such prohibition in the first two chapters of Genesis. Their precepts regarding human sexuality seem to be concerned with things that should be done rather than things that should not be done. If we feel that some prohibitions must be implied there too, I think we should ask ourselves whether we are coming to the text with an assumption that the default ethical value of sexual acts as such is that they are *bad* or *wrong* or *unclean*, and that something special, such as a divine purpose to which they are quite specifically fitted, is needed to make them appropriate and good. That hardly goes well with the claim of Genesis 1:31 that everything God had made was found to be 'very good' in God's sight. If we have a sense of our sexuality as dangerous, a sense that we *need* divine prohibitions in this area to give us good boundaries, that is understandable; and such fears will be discussed more fully in the final section of this paper. But fears need to be tamed if we are to listen openly and objectively to the Spirit that blows where it will.

The second chapter of Genesis suggests a second purpose of the creator for human sexuality, saying, 'Then the man said [of the woman], "This at last is bone of my bone and flesh of my flesh . . . " Therefore a man leaves his father and mother and clings to his wife, and they become one flesh' (Genesis 2:23-24). This passage says nothing about the possible or actual procreative effect of sexual intercourse. Rather it proposes a *unitive* purpose for what is clearly understood as a sexual relationship. The partners in this relationship are to cling so firmly to each other that they 'become one flesh'.

This is normally interpreted as referring to a marriage relation between a man and a woman. Jesus, famously, interpreted it as indicating God's purpose that such a relationship should be one of lifelong commitment and loyalty, not to be ended by divorce. The relationship of marriage is also viewed by biblical writers as meant to imitate, and thus offer insight into, God's relationship of love and commitment to Israel and to the Church (Hosea 2-3; Ephesians 5:28-33).

I am far from proposing to deny that such purposes for heterosexual marriage were part of God's aim in creating human sexuality. But the obvious question that confronts us here is whether they *exhaust* God's unitive purposes for human sexuality. Many same-sex couples argue that they realise the same values of committed, loyal, costly love in their unions, in which their sexuality is engaged. Why would that not fulfil much the same unitive purpose?

It may be objected that this proposal overlooks something very important. Genesis 2 gives us an account in which woman was created for man – and, by implication, it may now be added, man for woman. The fellowship intended here by God's creative purpose is specifically one of woman with man and man with woman. Again I agree that a friendship and partnership of the two sexes is intended in this biblical passage and very plausibly regarded as part of God's creative purpose. But surely the divinely purposed partnership between the sexes is not limited to marriage, let alone to sexual intercourse. There is no reliable evidence that Jesus, our new Adam, was married, and Christians have almost universally supposed that he was not. Is Jesus therefore in partnership only with men, and not equally with women? That would be sad news indeed for Christian women. And if partnership of the sexes is part of God's creative purpose for humanity, are celibate people to be exempted or excluded from it? But if celibate people can participate in the intended partnership of the sexes, why not homosexual people as well?

This is a point of fundamental importance – especially for women if they are to be freed by Christ from forms of bondage under which they have all too often laboured. If we believe, as St Paul said, that 'there is no male and female' for those who 'are one in Christ Jesus' (Galatians 3:28), we surely must suppose that the partnership of the sexes is not confined to the marriage relationship but has a primary place in the Church, and is not defined or limited by the obvious biological differences between the sexes, but enriches life together by all the diversities of experience and talents brought by individuals of both sexes. And if we think that way in the Church, should we not also suppose that the partnership of the sexes is to be fulfilled also in the workplace and in many other contexts of social relationship?

The term 'homosexuality' has been appropriated to refer to forms of preference and relationship that are sexual in a rather narrow and commonly physical sense; but we could also speak of 'social homosexuality', meaning patterns of personal and cultural preference that separate the sexes in many social contexts, and often exclude one sex or the other from some important realms of life. Such social homosexuality does not necessarily follow from, or accompany, physical or genital homosexuality, and it is obvious that it has very often characterised the social relationships of people who are physically and genitally heterosexual. And I believe it is the social rather than the more narrowly sexual or physical homosexuality that poses a serious threat to the partnership of the sexes, understood in the perspective of our all being one in Christ Jesus. Specifically, what so often leaves women treated as less than equal partners is not preferences about which sex to go to bed with, but fathers and brothers, teachers and bosses, who see children and siblings, students and supervisees, in living technicolour if they are male, and in unexciting black and white if they are female (except perhaps where a narrowly sexual partnership, or fantasy, is in view).

History and vocation

Creation narratives tend to focus our attention on the beginnings of humanity. If we seek guidance for sexual ethics there, we may be tempted to look for laws and institutions of fixed and unchangeable validity. But to what extent do we really believe that we can find in the beginnings of human society a permanently valid pattern for any social arrangement or institution? Not in any detail – not, at any rate, if we are among those who see in the first chapters of Genesis rich religious significance but not an accurate historical account of human origins. Even apart from Darwinian theories of *biological* evolution, we have plenty of reason to believe that human *society* has developed gradually, and that recognisably human beings lived long ago with no idea of a system of sexual relationships that any Christian would consider reasonable to put into practice today. The sexual as well as the political organisation of human society has always been in a process of change. This is not to say that such changes are all for the best. But in trying to evaluate actual and possible social changes we are likely to get more plausible guidance from visions of a better future than from ideas about an irrecoverable past. For such reasons Christian thought about

111

patterns of social relations, including sexual relations, should focus as much on eschatology as on creation.

But what do we know about the future? Where would we find an authentic vision of a better future? Christians will seek it in Christ, who calls us, not above all to stand by a primeval order of human life, but to embrace a reign of God in which all things are made new. I suggest that we would do well to think about such guidance in terms of *vocation*, and I propose that we think about vocation in terms of *goods that God offers us to love*.[2] This conception has, in my opinion, the following advantages.

1. Like the ideas of nature and creation, it focuses our attention on reality, on good gifts that God has actually given or offered to us, on goods that we can love in a future into which we see an actual path before us. It does not invite us to abandon actual goods for arbitrarily imagined ones, but rather to embrace and pursue divine gifts whose possibility and goodness we are convinced are real.

2. More clearly than the ideas of nature and creation, however, the idea of vocation points us toward the love of goods really possible in our own historical context, allowing us to recognise that those may not be just the same as the goods that God has offered to people in other times and places. A divine vocation is not an eternal law, but a command or invitation addressed to particular people in a particular context.

3. A vocation may, of course, be addressed to an individual, and Christian talk of vocation has very often been about individual vocations. We do not all necessarily have just the same vocation from God. It is not obvious that all Christians would have the same vocation in regard to their sexuality. Historically, indeed, it has been common to speak of some Christians having a vocation to celibacy and others to marriage; and the concept of vocation provides a framework in which we can express the thought that some Christians have a vocation to a same-sex life-partnership that includes sexual relations.

4. Whether that thought is right is not decided, of course, by a mere concept of vocation. A conception of vocation in terms of good gifts offered to us to love directs a Christian for whom the question is a live one to seek the aid of the

Holy Spirit in discerning whether such a same-sex partnership is indeed a good gift God is offering him or her. If we believe that the central goods Christ leads us to see in sexual relationship are those of faithful, self-giving love, I must say that I do not see why the answer about some same-sex partnerships would not be affirmative. In any case, the task of discernment to which the concept of vocation directs is not one we should reasonably expect to avoid. I believe that reasoning about nature or creation cannot rid us of it because we are not in a position to get very far in discerning divine purposes in nature or creation without presupposing judgements about what is good and right.

Notes

1 For an instructive essay that wrestles at length with these points, see William FitzPatrick, *Teleology and the Norms of Nature* (New York: Garland Publishing, 2000).
2 This conception of vocation is developed at greater length in Robert M. Adams, *Finite and Infinite Goods: A framework for ethics* (New York: Oxford University Press, 1999), Chapter 13.

7 Conversion – apparent and real

John Drury

> I beseech you therefore, brethren, by the mercies of God, that ye present your bodies a living sacrifice, holy, acceptable unto God, which is your reasonable service. And be not conformed to this world: but be ye transformed by the renewing of your mind, that ye may prove what is that good, and acceptable and perfect, will of God. (Romans 12:1-2)

It is a very commonplace and vexing fact that there is some sort of inherent lack, or contradiction in its own terms, about being human. Everyday language betrays it. Disappointment with other peoples' moral performances may provoke a resigned 'after all, they're only human', or the exasperation, in cases of idle or egocentric fantasy, of 'Join the human race!' – because getting above ourselves or making an exception of ourselves is the usual root of the trouble. Crooked timber. If we want to describe the sort of beings that we feel we ought to be, and which the circumstances of life cry out that we need to be, we add an 'e' and say 'humane'. This is defined by the dictionary as 'characterised by such behaviour or disposition towards others as befits a person: civil, courteous, obliging [epithets characteristically from the eighteenth century]; kind, benevolent [seventeenth century].' In other words, on a level of sensitivity with our neighbours.

The crucial territory or episode, then, is where 'human' changes into humane. For Emma Woodhouse it was in her carriage home from Box Hill.[1] It is where the gurus and philosophers, poets, novelists and gossips gather. They all tell us that this transition, even transformation, which matters to us so very much, is set with the tensions and transactions between the individual and society. Whatever else the lack may be – theologians will be ready with Original Sin and Newman's 'aboriginal calamity' – it certainly has to do with a weak sense of the reality of human society. This reality is something more elusive and problematic than its individuals expect or allow: even to the point of denying that there is such a thing, with results which still plague us. So it is with the individual, where the difficulty is felt, that inquiry into it can begin.

Everyone is a distinct centre of perception and feeling on to which everything converges, from which everything recedes. This is so ineluctable as to make us feel sometimes that we are imprisoned inside ourselves. But that is a bit hysterical. From where we are we can see a great deal and transmit all sorts of messages. And we can be seen and signalled to from outside. What matters is what our imaginations, accompanied by our wills, make of this. The centrality of the self is a given which imagining can turn to good or bad. It is the bad, the pathology, which first strikes everyday moralists. Here are two of them.

First, George Eliot explaining a 'pregnant little fact' with an illustration from Victorian domestic lighting:

> Your pier glass or extensive surface of polished steel made to be polished by a housemaid, will be minutely and multitudinously scratched in all directions; but place now against it a lighted candle as a centre of illumination, and lo! The scratches will seem to arrange themselves in a fine series of concentric circles round that little sun. It is demonstrable that the scratches are going everywhere impartially, and it is only your candle which produces the flattering illusion of a concentric arrangement, its light falling with an exclusive optical selection. These things are a parable. The scratches are events, and the candle is the egoism of any person now absent.[2]

Second, Simone Weil, also making central, but more insistent, use of the word 'illusion':

> Just as God, being outside the universe, is at the same time the centre, so each man imagines he is situated in the centre of the world. The illusion of perspective places him at the centre of space; an illusion of the same kind falsifies his idea of time; and

yet another kindred illusion arranges a whole hierarchy of values around him. The illusion is extended even to our sense of existence, on account of the intimate connection between our sense of value and our sense of being; being seems to us less and less concentrated the further it is removed from us.[3]

We are in trouble. Illusion is deeply set in us and brings the constant risk that, being on such poor terms with how things really are, we will blunder about and make things even worse than they are already for ourselves and other people. Every moment the examples crowd in. The people in front of me in the queue for the checkout need expect no mercy from my irate imagination, those who crowd the pavement are obstacles to be negotiated,

> and when night
> Darkens the streets, then wander forth the sons
> Of Belial, flown with insolence and wine[4]

to suggest fantasies about the use of a power hose. Ill myself, it cheers me up a bit and checks my self-pity, to notice that others are worse. And after a funeral it can be easy to feel with Pistol on his way to Falstaff's deathbed, 'We will condole the knight, but lambkins, we shall live.'[5] The serpent turns out to have been quite right about our being like gods, discerning between good and evil – in terms of each one's self-divinised position. Polytheism on this scale threatens all kinds of coherence.

We are not imprisoned in our skins, but we cannot jump out of them either. If we felt the distress, even of our nearest and dearest (all of it, all the time), as acutely as we feel our own, our social worlds would seize up and we would have to be led away. This is ineluctable. It is the illusion of centrality which is the trouble. And this, we have noticed, is a matter of the imagination, to which religion addresses itself. Can this trouble be relieved? Some lightly enforced socialising of the self, such as college or office life, might do that – if only superficially, still beneficially. So, more ambitiously and urgently, can it be cured? That is a taller order, needing, perhaps, supernatural grace. Which is where certain religious people, claiming to have just that, step in.

They have been vociferous recently. They were roused by

the prospect, since withdrawn, of a homosexual bishop of Reading and the actuality of one in New Hampshire. Although there have been plenty of homosexual bishops in the Church already, making it quite possible to assess their suitability for that office realistically and in detail, that was not at all the agenda. Secure in their own imaginations of their own possession of the Christian tradition and their standing under supernatural grace, they focussed their energies on accusing their more tolerant opponents of unprincipled surrender to the spirit of the age and, in the words of our text, being 'conformed to this world' rather than being 'transformed by the renewing of their minds' – of being estranged from 'what is that good and acceptable and perfect will of God'. Accusing the brethren is biblically the role of Satan. But, also biblically, Satan's accusations are made at the bar of truth. He and God agree on that. So is it true that these accusers are people whose minds, far from being conformed to this world, have been renewed and transformed into coherence with God's will?

In other words, have they been converted? They are apparently, and unlike cradle Christians or those who have absorbed their religion by some slow processes of osmosis, a society of converts. Their conversions were punctiliar and distinct. And unlike the outward formality and poetic ritual of the sacrament of baptism, they were located in intense inward emotions of desire and surrender. Once so converted, the convert makes the conversion of others as urgent a duty as staying within the group and sticking to its norms. Such emphasis should surely mark the real thing: a transition from the merely human to the thoroughly humane, a deliverance from the illusion of one's own central and special standing in the world and an enhanced sense of the reality of other people: a discontinuity, a transformation of the mind.

But that is not what they show us. New opinions, new friends, new ways of spending their time and, above all, the warmth of belonging to a cheerfully like-minded group instead of the loneliness of the shivering, hungry self – all that can be noticed. But so can a strong continuity, not discontinuity, with the moral attitudes of the unregenerate self. These are now shared with fellow believers and sanctified by a kind of group egocentricity. This is more comfortable, stronger and less anxious than the individual kind. The group, like the old self, senses itself to be special. It is convened by God, who is thanked for this favour and with whom it enjoys an intimate relationship of covenant. The title deeds of this covenant are in the Bible, a primary ligature between God and the group, which believes itself to be the direct addressee of all the sacred texts, and reads them accordingly. In principle, anyway. In practice there is a tendency to gravitate towards the gospel of St John, rather than the other three, because its highly concentric structure (as in Jesus' 'I am' sayings there and his parables of sheepfold and vine) suits the mentality of the group nicely. In principle, the whole of the book of Leviticus should, as covenanting word of God, be obeyed and enacted. In practice, a couple of verses interpreted as banning all and any homosexuality in the present day, are selected. Along with much else, the death penalty enjoined in the sacred text is politely ignored.

We are all prejudicially selective readers, so none of this is in the least surprising or alien to us. The thing is to be aware of this and aim off for it accordingly, as the great Church historian F. C. Baur acknowledged his Hegelianism as just what he would expect of himself as a mid-nineteenth-century historian. It is not so much as prejudicially selective readers, as self-unaware ones, that we are bad readers, sore let and hindered by our unregeneracy. We need to be rid of this so as to read as we should listen to other people, with open and alert attention and readiness to think again. This demands a positive attitude to texts, as having concerns other than our own; even a welcoming of a text's resistance to our prejudices as an enhancement and an opportunity for the renewing of our minds. A good reader has a sense of the differences between texts, of the individual particularity of each, just as a good person has of other people. By the same token, a good reader learns to read a text as addressed to people quite other than himself or his coterie. Dogma derived from treating all the texts as much of a muchness, which overwhelms the text's own context and concerns, defeats the very purpose of reading. And bad reading becomes something even worse, hypocritical reading, when we ignore our own partiality in reading so as to accuse other people of it, 'Why beholdest thou the mote that is in thy brother's eye and considerest not the beam that is in thine own eye? Thou hypocrite, first cast out the beam that is in thine own eye, and then shalt thou see clearly to cast the mote out of thy brother's eye.'[6]

How we read matters, and not just to ourselves. That religious people who set so much store by it, should do it so inattentively and then use it to such hostile purposes, is an evil. It threatens Christianity at its source. Christianity is under very serious threat from those who advertise themselves as its true converts and upholders, while displaying publicly all the familiar traits of the unconverted, untransformed self: egoism which believes itself exceptional, strong boundaries between itself and humanity at large, love of denunciation, bullying and hypocrisy. We can hope that the reckless display of all this will make it disreputable. But we must fear that its appeal to what is base in human nature by transposing it into a sanctimonious key, and presenting that deft continuity as a radical discontinuity, will find plenty of buyers from its stall at Vanity Fair.

Meanwhile we still stand in practical need of radical conversion – not once, but time and again. It is not available where it is stridently advertised. But that does not exhaust Christianity or its Scriptures, which survive and rebuke their bad readers. With the help of our text's contrasting criteria of conformity to the world and transforming renewal of the mind, we have been able to clear the ground of some rubbish. We still need to know what movement of the mind could take us from that conformity to that transformation. Back to the Bible.

Philippians 2 describes, using some necessarily mythological terms, the divine and inward movement by which this is effected.

> Look not everyone to his own things [it is Christians who are addressed] but everyone also on the things of others. Let this mind be in you, which was also in Christ Jesus: who, being in the form of God, thought it not a prize ['a piece of good fortune, a windfall' are other possible translations] to be grasped to be equal with God; but emptied himself, taking the form of a

119

servant, being born in the likeness of men. And being found in human form, he humbled himself and became obedient unto death, even death on a cross.

From a quite humdrum moral instruction, to make other people our concern, this famous text moves into a searching outreach and letting go, an unfulfilment or defulfilment, suffering and an outcast end. It is a journey of divinity into a far country, of the fortunate into misfortune, of the truly special into the utterly common. This is the very poetry of grace, distinguishing it from privilege or luck. And all to correct our everyday social transactions, where we should 'look everyone on the things of others'.

This is discontinuous. This goes against the grain of our unregeneracy. To which end, Thomas Traherne used a kind of flanking movement. One must realise, he taught, that just as one is 'the heir of all the world' and at its centre, so too is every other human being, 'all the supernumerary persons being enrichers of my inheritance'.[7] This increases felicity and so passes over the boundaries made by the self and the world's cultural constructions of division with a smiling ease. It also lets us into the enjoyment of reading, by which we escape from self into other lives and sympathies. So Traherne rejoiced in the sheer variety of the Scriptures, which bore him company in the good life of vivacious charity.

Simone Weil was more of a pessimist. She saw how difficult, how painfully against the grain, this crossing over or outreach can be in the face of the afflicted. We shun misfortune. That is nature. But the unfortunate need our affectionate attention to affirm their diminished personhood. That would be grace, which for her was exemplified in the story of how Parsifal attained the Holy Grail. Arrived, after long wanderings, at its shrine, and having it within his reach, he noticed its guardian, the sick Fisher King. At this point he forgot himself and his quest, turning to ask the wretched man what he was going through. And just that was the achievement of his quest, the accomplishment of his mission. The parable of the Good Samaritan and St Paul's hymn to charity teach the same lesson. Weil sharpened its edge. She wrote:

God is not present even if we invoke him, when the afflicted are merely regarded as an occasion for doing good. A man has all he can do [glossing the Good Samaritan], even if he concentrates all the attention of which he is capable, to look at the small, inert thing of flesh, lying stripped of clothing by the wayside. It is not the time to turn his thoughts to God. At such times, the presence of God in us has as its condition a secret so deep that it is a secret even to us. There are times when thinking of God separates us from him.

And, glossing the parable of the Sheep and the Goats this time ('Lord, when saw we thee naked or an-hungered?') she adds 'He who gives bread to the famished sufferer for the love of God will not be thanked by Christ. He has already had his reward in the thought itself. Christ thanks those who do not know to whom they are giving food.'[8] The exegesis is faithful there, the sense of supernatural grace, strong. Proprietary religion is exploded by the priority of charity, of understanding and of grace. We are left with plenty to do and enough indication of how to do it well: a more excellent, if narrow, way to follow. More excellent than what? Well, no need to go over all that again. We can conclude and set out again by standing momentarily with Bunyan's Pilgrim at the start of his journey when, troubled by his reading, he meets Evangelist.

> Then said Evangelist, pointing with his finger over a very wide field, Do you see yonder wicket-gate? The man said, No. Then said the other, Do you see yonder shining light? He said, I think I do. Then said Evangelist, keep that light in your eye, and go up directly thereto, so shalt thou see the gate; at which, when thou knockest, it shall be told thee what thou shalt do.[9]

This essay was published in *Theology*, November/December 2004

Notes

1 Jane Austen, *Emma*, Vol. III, Chapter 7.
2 George Eliot, *Middlemarch*, Chapter 27.
3 Simone Weil, 'Forms of the Implicit Love of God' in *Waiting on God* (Routledge and Kegan Paul, 1951), p.98.
4 Milton, *Paradise Lost*, I, lines 500ff.

5 Shakespeare, *Henry V*, II, i.
6 Matthew 7:3-5.
7 Thomas Traherne, *Centuries*, I, 15.
8 Simone Weil, *Waiting on God* (Routledge and Kegan Paul, 1951), pp.91-2.
9 John Bunyan, *The Pilgrim's Progress* I.

Appendix

The Church of England: Decades of debate

The first official report, *Homosexual Relationships: A contribution to discussion*[1] in 1979, chaired by the then Bishop of Gloucester John Yates, was thought too liberal, and a Foreword was added by the Board of Social Responsibility arguing that it did not do justice to biblical teaching. The report began with the setting of a radically changed society which assumed that most people were sexually active, but stated 'we know very little about the majority of homosexual men and women'. The working party believed that 'for many people sexual preference is not a matter of stark alternatives, but is to be found somewhere on a continuum between an exclusive preference for sexual relationships with one's own sex and an equally exclusive preference for sexual relationships with the opposite sex'. The report acknowledged that 'at present, medical science can give only a very incomplete account of the formation of sexual orientation. What we do know suggests that people have the responsibility for deciding whether or not to express their orientation in sexual acts, though the very strong nature of the sexual drive must be reckoned with'. That final concessive clause is of considerable importance. Undoubtedly *Homosexual Relationships* moved towards the acceptance of homosexuality as a 'given fact', though not giving it equality with heterosexual partnerships, but it lacked a full and accurate study of homosexual men and women, and not simply those who publicly declare their homosexuality. In addressing biblical evidence, it noted 'Even when we can be confident that our text of the Bible is fixed and constant, the Church's understanding and use of it, and hence the attitudes and actions which derive from this, are not.' The report went on 'The appeal to Scripture, if it is to be illuminating, must look to the biblical treatment of the central themes of human love and marriage rather than to the occasional and somewhat peripheral texts that mention homosexuality itself; and the appeal to nature must be made in a broader context than the merely biological.'

The Board of Social Responsibility's cautionary Foreword over the signature of Bishop Graham Leonard said 'We do believe that the Report and the attached critical comments can make an important contribution to the process of forming the mind of the church. We therefore envisage a period during which widespread discussion takes place.' General Synod commended the report with the Foreword for discussion in diocesan and deanery synods. Little formal discussion took place.

In 1987 the General Synod debated[2] a private member's motion by the Revd Tony Higton, that

> This Synod reaffirms the biblical standard, given for the well-being of society:
> (i) that sexual intercourse should take place only between a man and a woman who are married to each other;
> (ii) that fornication, adultery and homosexual acts are sinful in all circumstances;
> (iii) that Christian leaders are called to be exemplary in all spheres of morality, including sexual morality, as a condition of being appointed to or remaining in office;
> (iv) and calls upon the Church to show Christ-like compassion to those who have fallen into sexual sin, encouraging them to repent and receive absolution, and offering the ministry of healing to all who suffer physically or emotionally as a result of such sin.

The debate took place under intense media scrutiny. Several amendments were debated. In the end the Synod voted overwhelmingly that:

> This Synod affirms that the biblical and traditional teaching on chastity and fidelity in personal relationships is a response to,

and expression of, God's love for each one of us, and in particular affirms:

(1) that sexual intercourse is an act of total commitment which belongs properly within a permanent married relationship,

(2) that fornication and adultery are sins against this ideal, and are to be met by a call to repentance and the exercise of compassion,

(3) that homosexual genital acts also fall short of this ideal, and are likewise to be met by a call to repentance and the exercise of compassion,

(4) that all Christians are called to be exemplary in all spheres of morality, including sexual morality, and that holiness of life is particularly required of Christian leaders.

The Osborne Report to the House of Bishops in 1989, drawing on direct testimony from Christian homosexuals, has never been allowed to be published, though its findings were eventually leaked to the media. Evidently it was even-handed but suggested that the Church needed to be more welcoming to gay people. 'We need to keep clearly in mind that if what we stand for makes no connection with the real dilemmas and questions experienced by homosexual people we are in danger of failing in the basic pastoral task.'

In 1991 the Bishops published their own report, *Issues in Human Sexuality*,[3] commended for discussion in dioceses as part of an educational process, acknowledging that it was 'not the last word on the subject'. The prevailing nervousness, however, seriously restricted much debate in official Church bodies, in synods and church councils. The level of nervousness is illustrated by the fact that a deanery clergy reading group in the North East, having sent to Lambeth Palace their 1000-word response composed in 1992 after several study sessions, despite repeated requests could get no acknowledgement even that it had been received. It was not until 1997 that the General Synod debated *Issues in Human Sexuality* and officially supported its commendation for discussion.

There was debate in other places. In 1993 the *Christian Action Journal* devoted an issue to *Intimacy and Sexuality*[4] but its circulation was limited and it will not have reached most parts of the Church. It contained ten valuable articles including one by Christopher Rowland on 'Jesus, the Gospels and Intimacy'. Gillian Orchard, a religious Sister of the Institute of the Blessed Virgin Mary, wrote about celibacy as a singular freedom, nothing to do with sexlessness or lack of passion, nor with lack of feeling or not needing companions, affirmation and affection. Elaine Graham from the University of Manchester writing on 'Gender and Intimacy' suggested that intimacy born of similarity, fellowship and shared interest should lead into, rather than prevent, a more generous vision of reaching beyond the boundaries of security towards a broader notion of community. Chris Rowland warned of abuses of power, saying 'Intimacy without some understanding of the boundaries involved risks, exploitation, manipulation and hurt.' Together these insights provided a necessary corrective to those Christians who considered interest in issues of human sexuality to be a narrow 'obsession with sex', of relevance only to a minority.

In its 1990 issue, entitled 'Widening the Horizons: Towards more christian action on fear, stress and sex',[5] the *Christian Action Journal* contained articles by Eric James, David Lewis, James Woodward, Jeffrey John, John Lee and Leslie Houlden. It was particularly concerned with the stress experienced by homosexual clergy, though it recognised that the stress could not be divided from that suffered by homosexual people in general. John Baker and Robin Green contributed reviews of Dr Ben Fletcher's book *Clergy under Stress: A study of homosexual and heterosexual clergy in the Church of England.*[6]

In 1995 came Michael Vasey's *Strangers and Friends: A new exploration of homosexuality and the Bible.*[7] He described it as a continued attempt to hear and understand the Bible, aiming to help both 'those who come to the subject fairly fresh and also people who are reasonably familiar with the complex arguments that the subject has gathered to itself'. Looking at sexuality, nature and culture, and at what is involved in making judgements in these areas, Vasey provided a detailed map which could help people make sense of this complex subject and how it relates to Christian faith.

As a gay person writing from an evangelical standpoint, his book made a particular impact.

In the same year the St Andrew's Day Statement was produced by 'a group of theologians concerned at the fevered conflict over homosexuality gripping the Church'. That is how the group which produced the St Andrew's Day Statement was described in 1997 by their chairman in *The Way Forward?*,[8] a book of essays from all sides of the debate. Far from having a neutral starting point as is sometimes claimed, the group which wrote the St Andrew's Day Statement met at the request of the Church of England Evangelical Council. Its authors shared a particular theological standpoint as to the incontrovertible claims of Scripture which would not be how all believers would wish to approach the Bible. Nevertheless, the authors of *The Way Forward?* included theologians from a range of positions: Rowan Williams, Oliver O'Donovan, Jeffrey John, Anthony Thistelton, Michael Vasey and Tim Bradshaw. It was a volume intended as a resource for 'all concerned about the questions at issue, who want the full range of opinion but who want dialogue rather than diatribe'.

The Lambeth Conference of Anglican Communion Bishops in 1998 in its sub-group studying human sexuality was unable to reach a common mind on the 'scriptural, theological, historical and scientific issues'.[9] The full Conference, after fierce debate and with one-sixth of those present dissenting or abstaining, rejected homosexual practice as incompatible with Scripture, committed themselves as bishops to listen to the experience of homosexual persons, and called on all Anglicans to

> minister pastorally and sensitively to all regardless of sexual orientation and to condemn irrational fear of homosexuals, violence within marriage and any trivialisation and commercialisation of sex.

The Lambeth Conference was followed closely by *A Pastoral Statement to Lesbian and Gay Anglicans from Some Member Bishops of the Lambeth Conference*,[10] apologising that within the limitations of the Conference, it had not been possible to hear adequately their voices and to reflect theologically and spiritually upon their lives and ministries. The signatory bishops called for continuing, prayerful, respectful conversation.

Another response to the Lambeth Conference was the initiative of Bishop Steven Charleston from Cambridge, Massachusetts, in drawing up *The Cambridge Accord*[11] for bishops to sign. By 2000, bishops from the USA, Canada, Puerto Rico, Honduras, Cyprus and the Gulf, South Africa, Melanesia, New Zealand, and Australia had done so, as had 22 bishops from England, Scotland and Wales, including the new Archbishop of Canterbury, Rowan Williams.

The Cambridge Accord, while recognising that bishops 'have divergent views on the "biblical, theological and moral" issues surrounding homosexuality' invited them to stand in unity on three essential points, the key points of the Accord:

a. that no homosexual person should ever be deprived of liberty, property or civil rights because of his or her sexual orientation;

b. that all acts of violence, oppression and degradation against homosexual persons are wrong and cannot be sanctioned by an appeal to the Christian faith;

c. that every human being is created equal in the eyes of God and therefore deserves to be treated with dignity and respect.

The Cambridge Accord had begun by recognising that 'the global persecution of homosexuals has reached alarming proportions' and that, because the Anglican Church's debates about homosexuality had recently been in the limelight, 'the responsibility for us to calm the passions of hate have become even more acute.'

True Union in the Body,[12] commissioned in 2002 by the Archbishop of the West Indies and written by two tutors at Wycliffe Hall (an evangelical Anglican theological college in Oxford) primarily to address the Anglican Communion discussion of the public blessing of same-sex unions, moved the debate forward to a wide-ranging study of the sweeping themes of Scripture, but based initially on Genesis 1 to 3. It can be argued that Scripture offers other starting-points which lead to different conclusions, and also that our way of understanding Scripture can lead to a very different approach.

In 2003 the House of Bishops published *Some Issues in Human Sexuality: A guide to the debate*[13] together with *A Companion*, a study guide on how to use *Some Issues*. *Some Issues* works within the parameters of the 1991 *Issues* report. Its Foreword states that it 'does not seek to change the position of the House of Bishops from the one established there'. Rather it seeks to help people enter into the ensuing debate.

Some Issues tries to help all who are likely to find debate difficult, both those for whom any challenging of Scripture is painful and those for whom this is a debate which touches closely on their own identity and integrity, particularly expressed in sexuality, but in making this attempt it quickly reverts to an evangelical position drawing heavily on themes discerned in Genesis 1 to 3. It quotes Archbishop Carey's words commending the International Anglican Conversations on Human Sexuality, a report from twelve Anglican leaders meeting for three years after the 1998 Lambeth Conference:

> We use dialogue in order to clarify where misunderstandings may lie; to probe deeper into the motives for adopting this or that position in regard to certain issues; and to appreciate better (even though we may not agree with them) the reasons why some people's views differ so radically from our own. In this way our deeper search for truth will not be divorced from the fellowship we need for truth to emerge.

Their report itself said:

> We discovered in our own experience the importance of 'Interpretive charity': imputing the best intentions to our colleagues and other members of our communion, telling the better stories about them, checking (if possible at first hand) before drawing conclusions.

Notes

1 *Homosexual Relationships: A contribution to discussion* (CIO, 1979).
2 The full record of the debate is printed in General Synod Report of Proceedings vol. 18:3 (Church House Publishing, 1987), pp.913-56.
3 *Issues in Human Sexuality* (Church House Publishing, 1991).

4 *Christian Action Journal,* summer 1993.

5 *Christian Action Journal,* summer 1990.

6 Ben Fletcher, *Clergy under Stress: A study of homosexual and heterosexual clergy* (Mowbray, 1990).

7 Michael Vasey, *Strangers and Friends: A new exploration of homosexuality and the Bible* (Hodder & Stoughton, 1995).

8 Timothy Bradhsaw (ed.), *The Way Forward: Christian voices on homosexuality and the Church* (Hodder & Stoughton, 1997).

9 *The Official Report of the Lambeth Conference 1998* (Morehouse Publishing, 1999).

10 *A Pastoral Statement to Lesbian and Gay Anglicans from Some Member Bishops of the Lambeth Conference:* http://justus.anglican.org/resources/Lambeth 1998/paststmnt.html

11 *The Cambridge Accord:* www.episdivschool.edu/abouteds/cambridgeaccord.htm

12 Peter Walker and Andrew Goddard, *True Union in the Body,* a contribution to the discussion within the Anglican Communion concerning the public blessing of same-sex unions. Published jointly by the Anglican Institute (Colorado, USA) and the Oxford consultation on *The Future of Anglicanism* (July 2002).

13 *Some Issues in Human Sexuality: A guide to the debate* (Church House Publishing, 2003).

Index